my life with johnny ramone

# Too Tough to Love

## CYNTHIA "ROXY" WHITNEY
### and emily xyz

❧
new green press

ISBN #978-0-9963724-1-1

Address inquiries to:
newgreenpress@gmail.com

*Cover Photo: Johnny Ramone and Cynthia Whitney at WWF restling,*
*Rosemont Horizon, Rosemont IL, September 1986*
*© Richard Whitney*

# Contents

Foreword............................v

Acknowledgements........................ix

1975........................15

1973–74–75........................19

1976........................43

1977........................71

1978........................112

1979........................117

1980........................123

1981........................137

1982........................154

1983........................156

1984–89........................167

1990–98........................177

2003–04........................198

2010........................211

2011........................216

Epilogue: Dominatrix........................218

Notes........................225

About the Authors........................247

# Foreword

BY NOW MOST RAMONES FANS have heard the story of betrayal at the heart of their beloved band: how guitarist Johnny stole singer Joey's girlfriend Linda, and how Johnny and Joey never dealt with it, or each other, for the rest of the group's long career. What is not so well known is that the love triangle had a fourth side: Johnny's longtime girlfriend, Cynthia "Roxy" Whitney.

Most Ramones histories and memoirs (including the otherwise-great documentary *End of the Century*, and Johnny's own posthumously published autobiography, *Commando*) either leave Roxy out completely or mention her only in passing, usually dismissing her as a drunk, one of the "crazy girls" that hung around the band. She has never been interviewed for any Ramones or punk rock book, article, or film. Yet she was Johnny's live-in partner, lover, confidante and companion for seven years—the first seven years of punk, when the Ramones were at the forefront of a revolution in rock and at the height of their creative power and influence—and remained intimately connected with him for fourteen more years after that.

Roxy's affair with Johnny Ramone began in early 1976, around the time the Ramones' first album was released. The following year they moved into an apartment in New York's East Village, where they lived together for the next six and a half years. For most of that time, Johnny was still legally married to his first wife. Roxy left New York in 1983, but her relationship with Johnny continued until January 1998. By then, Johnny had been married to Linda Daniele for several years.

Linda had been the girlfriend of Johnny's bandmate, singer Joey Ramone, for two years when she and Johnny started their affair in secret in 1979. The betrayal caused deep rifts among all concerned: Roxy cut ties with her former friend; Linda disappeared from the Ramones camp; Joey and Johnny stopped speaking to each other, even as the band continued to tour and record for another 14 years.

Linda finally abandoned Joey for Johnny in 1982, but Johnny did not leave Roxy, despite the claim made in his autobiography. He never admitted his involvement with Linda to Joey and steadfastly denied it to Roxy, even as he and Linda took a place together just a few blocks away. Years later, *Commando* compounded the insult, downplaying and essentially erasing his entire relationship with Roxy—and of course, never mentioning their ongoing contact for years after he and Linda were together and even married.

After a near-fatal assault on Johnny in August 1983, Roxy went home to Chicago, intending to stay only briefly; but she never returned to live with him again. Their relationship continued, however, in the form of daily calls, financial support, and frequent gifts and "care packages" from him, as well as occasional visits. In 1990, Roxy moved to Los Angeles. She worked for a while in TV and film but eventually became a professional dominatrix. Johnny and Linda were married in 1994; two years later, in May 1996, they also moved to Los Angeles, where the Ramones played their last show on August 6. By then, Roxy had begun a long downward spiral of drug abuse and criminal activity. She was arrested in January 1998 and went to prison in California, at which point her involvement with Johnny, and his financial support of her, finally ended. That summer, Johnny began radiation treatment for the prostate cancer that would claim his life six years later.

Following several periods of incarceration, Roxy was released in May 2009 and resumed working as a dominatrix in the Los Angeles area under the name Mistress Sin. She went to prison again in 2013, and has recently been training to work as a cosmetologist after her release. Johnny's widow, who goes by the name Linda Ramone, also still lives in Los Angeles, manages his estate, shares responsibility (with Joey's brother Mickey Leigh) for administering Ramones-related business, and occasionally appears in the media in support of right-wing causes.

The interviews and correspondence with Cynthia Whitney that make up this book were conducted between 2006–15. This is the first time she has spoken publicly about her relationship with Johnny Ramone and, except for minor elisions for clarity, it is her story entirely in her own words. Additional research and quoted material from other sources is presented in the sidebars and Notes as supporting documentation for Roxy's version of events.


emily xyz
Ann Arbor MI / Saratoga Springs NY
April 2015

# Acknowledgements

**Cynthia Whitney** would like to thank Gyda Gash, Anya Phillips, Eileen Polk, Lyn Todd, Arthur Kane, Louie Scorcia, Luigi Ruggiero, Eliott Kidd Cohen, Irma Ruiz, Elida Ramirez, Malcolm McLaren; Dee Dee Ramone, Joey Ramone, Tommy Ramone, Marky Ramone, Vera Ramone, Marion Flynn, Claudia Tienan, Connie Gripp, Danny Fields, Linda Stein, Monte Melnick, Mitch and Arlene, the Ramones crew, Doris & Boris, Missy L and the gang; James Chance, Howie Pyro, Johnny Angel Wendell, Ken Chang, Tom Shoard, Michael Mabe, Douglas "Jack" Kevorkian, Joseph Englert, Nico Hill, David Hynes, Brett Ericson, Jesse Rosenfeld, Michelle "Red" Newman, Mike Wilson, David Sutcliffe and Robert Mulé; my sister Carolyn and my brother Richard; my parents, Emerson Whitney and Eileen Holmberg Whitney; Johnny's parents, Frank Cummings and Estelle (Stella) Krasig Cummings; Johnny Ramone; and Emily XYZ.

**Emily XYZ** would like to thank Gyda Gash, Eileen Polk, Ann Henderling, Monte Melnick, Danny Fields, Andy Schwartz, John Holmstrom, Legs McNeil, Vera Ramone, Johnny Angel Wendell, Richard Whitney, Robert Mulé, William Krasilovsky, Rob Wallis, Rick Moody, Richard Pine, Gillian McCain, Jon Galt, Michael Grant, Josh Katz, Melissa Beck, John Sullivan and Julie Fink Sullivan, Wayne Tobias, Jenny Meyer, Cate Grund, Myers Bartlett, Kim Osburn, and my sister, Mary Laurents, for information, advice, encouragement and support; Jesse Atwell for research and formatting assistance; the Fales Collection at Bobst Library, NYU; the New York Public Library; the music library at the School of Music, Theatre and Dance, University of Michigan/Ann Arbor; The Ramones; and most of all, Cynthia Whitney, a/k/a Roxy.

my life with johnny ramone

# Too Tough to Love

*Isn't it funny how you can be obliterated out of history? Roxy was made out to be the bad guy and the crazy person. But they needed people like that, they sucked that shit dry and made art out of it and then they just, "Oh we don't know them, they're too" — like, we're too crazy. Well, that's what your fuckin whole art is about! You should be fuckin paying homage to that!*

*— Gyda Gash, musician*

*Many women have just been written out of history and then Punk gets a false reputation as being male-oriented. Do people really believe that all those guys were there because there weren't any women?*

*— Eileen Polk, photographer*

14

# 1975

I FIRST MET JOHNNY RAMONE at Performance Studio in September 1975, at a show they were playing with Blondie. Anya Phillips and I had just gotten back to New York from England, and she knew Debbie Harry from White's Pub, a go-go bar on Wall Street where they both worked. Anya said, "We have to go see my friend Debbie, and there's this other band that's playing, the Ramones." She said, "You gotta see them, you'd really like 'em." So we went.

Performance Studio was where the Ramones got their start, it was the first place they ever played. It was just a small room, I think it was a rehearsal studio. I'd never been there before and I don't think I ever went back.

Performance Studios Ltd., a rehearsal and performance venue at 23 East 20th Street, was co-operated by musicians Tommy Erdelyi, later known as Tommy Ramone, the Ramones' original drummer and producer, and Monte Melnick, later the Ramones' road manager. The Ramones played their first-ever show there on March 30, 1974, as a trio, and continued to rehearse and perform there through 1974 and '75. The venue was also the site of the last New York Dolls rehearsals, in summer 1975 (with

singer David Johansen and guitarist Sylvain
Sylvain only, after the band's breakup in April
and prior to Johansen and Sylvain playing
several dates in Japan). The shows with Blondie
on September 12 and 13, 1975, including the
one that Roxy and Anya attended, would be the
last times the Ramones played at Performance
Studios. The studio closed in early 1976.

*Performance Studios was on the second floor.
The elevator was small, rickety and old. Not
quite sure on the color of the main room now
but it was a dark color and the walls were
draped in fabric (for acoustic dampening). We
had fluorescent lights and stage lighting for
shows. No curtain, just a small two foot high
stage in the back of the room. Performance
Studios was located on 20th Street not far
from the famous Max's Kansas City Club.
It was across the street from Theodore
Roosevelt's Birthplace.   — Monte Melnick*

I just remember standing there and watching...just Johnny. I was
mesmerized by Johnny. I liked the way he looked, I liked the way he
moved. He looked tough. And he looked cool.

Anya and I were in full regalia, wearing ripped, safety-pinned clothes that we made ourselves. Slogans on our T-shirts, buttons from different British bands, mini-skirts, boots, stockings, Crazy Color hair—the look that later became punk style, but nobody was wearing it yet. I think there were a lot of musicians there, too, but it was like that all the time. They all liked me and Anya, and it was very cool because we were there!

We talked to him after the show. I told Anya, "I really love that guitar player!" She said, "Oh, you gotta go tell him! Go on, go on, go on, tell him, tell him!" and she was pushing me to go talk to him and tell him I thought he was hot. I was a little drunk or something and I guess I walked up to him and told him, "I love you." And this woman who was standing next to him said, "So do I, *honey!*" in this thick accent. She turned out to be his wife. I looked at Anya and she was, like, giggling in the background.

His wife finally walked away and Johnny came over and started talking to me. He knew Anya from somewhere, I think. He saw my Bay City Rollers pins and asked me if I liked them and I said yeah. He was grinning at me and we were talking about England and the Bay City Rollers and Slade and who's that band that did the "Ballroom Blitz"? [*Sweet*]. It was coming up to my birthday, I remember telling him about my birthday and he said, "Oh, well, my birthday's coming up, too," and it turned out we almost had the same birthday. He's October 8, I'm October 4.

I thought he was a nice guy. Friendly. He was cute, he was hot. He sounded intelligent, like he *thought*. And he was knowledgeable about music. He was what I was looking for, he was my type. I always like a tough, rough guy and Johnny fit the category. But I couldn't give him my phone number because his wife finally stopped him from talking to me. She was an Egyptian Jew—Rosana Choukrane was her name. He had one girlfriend before her, and that was Arlene, who ended up going out with Joey Ramone's brother, Mitch [*Mickey Leigh*]. Rosana hung around after she and Johnny broke up, too, she went out with somebody from

Mitch's band for a while, I think. Or somebody who was associated with the band, I forget his name. So it was like a big happy family all the time, everybody stuck pretty close.

I really liked the Ramones a lot. They were different from anything else that was going on at the time. I mean, Anya and I were very very big Sparks fans back then! We would go anywhere to see the Sparks, to meet them. We finally met them in Chicago and partied with them in New York, too, they had a party at Burger King [*also in 1975, shortly before this*]. That's where I first saw Linda Daniele.

But that night, I didn't talk to anybody else in the band, I just talked to Johnny. Later on he told me that what he noticed about me when he first met me were my breasts. That's what he liked about me. He liked big breasts. He really loved sexy bitches, big boobs—like *Playboy* material. That's why I couldn't understand years later how he ended up with Linda, unless she had some surgery...maybe she did. She needed it!

# 1973–74–75

*Anya told me that Roxy came from a wealthy
Chicago family, and Anya said that the big ring
Roxy wore was a real diamond.  — Eileen Polk*

SUPPOSEDLY THE RUMOR around New York was that I was an
heiress of the Vanderbilt-Whitney family. That sounds good to me! But
it's not true.

I'm originally from Chicago. My father's name was Emerson
Calhoun Whitney, my mother was Swedish, Eileen Holmberg was her
name. She was his second wife and was much younger than him. And I
have two brothers, one's older and one's younger—Richard and Kent—
and a sister, Carolyn. I had a step-brother also, and later on of course my
spiritual brother, Nico (*retired cage fighter Nico "The Dragon" Hill*).

My father was a visionary and was my hero growing up. He was
born in Oklahoma in 1910 and was related to Sam Houston and to Eli
Whitney, the cotton gin inventor. His father had been an artist and his
mother an exotic dancer. He and his older brother Eugene had both had
Hollywood screen contracts back in the early days of motion pictures
because they were quite handsome. My father put himself through
Northwestern University and became an attorney, then decided to go
into politics. He ran for the senate in Illinois but lost because of an

indiscretion that produced a child out of wedlock. His alcoholic first wife, when she found out, tried to kill him and herself. She tried the same thing again later, after she found out about him and my mother.

Eventually my father became an entrepreneur and was very successful. He had an interest in a steel company, that's where he met my mother—she was his secretary—and he was involved in an oil company, and he owned a lot of property in different areas of the United States, in Florida, New York, Pennsylvania I believe, Seattle, Texas, Mississippi. We lived in many of these places at different times. We always had a place in Chicago, but we traveled a lot by car. My father liked to drive and so we would go and live in these different properties for periods of time. One year we moved down to Texas in the summer, which is like the worst time to go live in Texas! Eventually my parents wanted us kids in a permanent school for some sort of stability, so my two brothers and I started living with my grandmother on the southeast side of Chicago.

My father would take us on nice vacations, too, like to Europe, the Caribbean, the Greek Islands. He loved to travel and wanted to go everywhere before he died. He was an insomniac, like I am. He and my mother were about twenty years apart in age and as he got older he slept less and less, he would be up walking around all night. He had a big library and he'd have his blackout curtains drawn and he would just sit up and read, and I'd go in and sleep with him sometimes—or stay up with him!

My father taught me a lot. He guided me and always told me that women are equal to men and that I could be anything I wanted to be, and to never give up on my dreams. He was very supportive, both my parents were supportive of us kids. I had a good relationship with my parents.

One of the things my father invested in was the Aragon Ballroom, a huge old dance hall in downtown Chicago that was built during Prohibition. It held thousands of people and my father saw its potential for making millions off the hippie generation and rock music. All the

big groups of the time came through there and I met them all as a shy
12-year old kid. It was such a thrill! That's where I got my first taste
for rock stars. No one could believe that my father owned the place and
was responsible for acts like Janis Joplin, Steppenwolf, Joe Cocker, Iron
Butterfly, Buffalo Springfield and Alice Cooper coming to town and
playing for exuberant, drugged-out hippie Chicagoans.

While I was in high school at Broadmoor Academy, I worked at the
Aragon box office, selling tickets. I had always loved music and wanted
to be part of that life. My mother didn't particularly like me working
nights till 4:00 a.m., driving home with my dad in his Cadillac with
briefcases stuffed with cash and his gun under the seat. No one was going
to rip Emerson C. Whitney off! He loved money and he loved his life.
He lived everything in a big way. He was a big man with big appetites.
He sold the Aragon to a group of New York investors who turned it into
a discotheque called the Cheetah Club. That didn't fly, so he ended up
taking it back and ran it for a few more years, until he died in 1973,
and then my mother sold it. She was not interested in it, but I sure was!
I wish she would have kept it for me. That would have been my life. I
would have had something to do that I really loved, putting on rock 'n'
roll shows and meeting the bands.

When I was 14 I hooked up with my first boyfriend. He was 17
and worked for my father, either at the Aragon or one of the slum hippie
buildings he owned. My father had warned me to stay away from these
boys, and that was all I needed to hear—those were the boys I went after.
He was a drug-dealing junkie dropout sicko sadist and I was fascinated
with him. He looked like how I pictured Jesus Christ—beautiful. He
taught me all about sex, which included beatings if I didn't do something
the way he wanted, or if he didn't have his heroin in the morning, or just
for the hell of it. He would fuck me in front of his friends, make me get
down on my knees and suck him off, then laugh at me, and he beat me
if I so much as looked at another guy. But it turned me on when he beat

me. I was petrified, scared to death, and *loving it!* In my mind, sex and violence equaled love, and that was all I had to base it on at the time. My mother saw the bruises on my arms and said, "You know, some people like that sort of thing." I know! I was one of them.

That relationship had a huge influence on my life. My girlfriends thought I was crazy. BDSM was not at all talked about like it is now, since *50 Shades of Gray.* It was still completely underground. I didn't understand it myself until years later, when I came across *The Story of O* and realized I was not the only one in the world who was into pain and pleasure.

I started drinking when I was 14, too. I knew from my first beer that I was an alcoholic, when I woke up at the beach by Lake Michigan. That's why I loved amphetamines, first pills and later crystal meth. It seemed like there was something lacking in my body and amphetamines made it right. They also afforded me a way to drink the way I liked to and never get drunk. *What a great drug!* I thought.

⌘

I graduated high school two years early and enrolled in Loyola University in September 1972, right before I turned 16. I made it through freshman year, but then at some point I remember one of my friends in Chicago showed me the *Star* magazine with L.A. teen groupies like Sable Starr, Queenie and Lori Maddox on the cover, and I figured Hollywood was the place for me. So I decided to go out to California with my friend Irma Ruiz. We got on one of those hotlines they used to have, where you could share a ride, and we drove out here to Los Angeles with some nut who we found out was delivering explosives to

San Diego. It was some hippie thing, I guess—gonna blow something up! We got out in Laguna Beach, wearing our glitter and lamé clothes from Granny Takes A Trip and Jumpin' Jack Flash, and hopped a bus for Hollywood.

Irma and I had a photographer friend in L.A., a guy named Bill Edmondson—"Sick Bill," as he was called—and we just moved in on him. His place was like a block from the Whisky, so we were hanging out there and at the Rainbow Club, getting drunk every night. Went to see The Stooges and a bunch of other bands. I liked it out here. The little tramps from *Star* mainly hung out at Rodney's English Disco, but Irma and I preferred the adult crowd at the Rainbow, especially the private club upstairs, where the elite hung out. Soon we were going to Hollywood Hills parties, fucking local talent like Zolar X, and having a blast.

My mother arranged for me to live in a studio apartment across Sunset Boulevard from the Continental Hyatt House—the "Riot House"—where there was always a lot of action. It was wild there, and I would find myself locked in a bathroom with a famous British rock star, or some local wanna-be, groping me. Such fun! Everyone was fucking everyone. This was before AIDS and Hep-C, when the worst thing that could happen was the clap, which could be dispensed with by one injection. Back then I looked like David Bowie on quaaludes, short red hair and far-out, spacey costumes interspersed with retro '40s Hollywood glamour—boas, fishnets and veils.

Then one day in July, the police came to my door. I guess we didn't have a telephone, because my mother sent the police to tell me to call her right away, that something had happened. When I called her, she said my father had died of a heart attack in Texas and that I was to come home immediately. So I went back to Chicago.

My childhood dreams were shattered when my father died. He was such a source of strength in our family. He left us money, but it did not compare to his mind and presence. I think my younger sister never got over it, and my mother sort of lost it, too. That's when I first started noticing her mood swings. Her manic-depression started running rampant after my father died, and I really wanted to get away from that. And she was trying to get rid of me, too. So I came back to L.A. pretty much right away, this time to go to school, supposedly, at the Fashion Institute of Design and Merchandising. Then I met the New York Dolls at the Whisky.

We went crazy when they came out! Sable was ready to pounce. I had a huge crush on Frenchy, their valet, but I ended up hanging with Arthur Kane. This was right after Connie stabbed Arthur—his hand was bandaged and he couldn't play. Peter Jordan played for him.

After wrapping up six nights at Max's Kansas City in New York, August 22–27, 1973, the New York Dolls were about to leave for their first shows in California, starting at the Whisky in Los Angeles, August 30–September 3. On (probably) August 28, bassist Arthur Kane's girlfriend Connie Gripp, angry that she would not be going to California with him, attacked Kane with a knife while he was asleep. In the ensuing struggle, Kane's right hand was cut so badly that he was unable to play the California shows. Nevertheless, the band left on schedule and played the dates with Dolls roadie Peter Jordan filling in on bass as Kane stood onstage nearby. Connie later became the girlfriend of Ramones bassist and songwriter Dee Dee Ramone, who immortalized her in songs like "Glad to See You Go" and "You're Gonna Kill That Girl." [1]

After the Dolls, I became fascinated with everything and anyone from New York. Then the school had a field trip to New York and that was it for me—as soon as I got there, I knew that's where I belonged. I had a New York boyfriend at that point, Louie Scorcia, who later ended up playing with Johnny Thunders. He was also a great photographer and I loved his accent and his wise-guy demeanor. He got me to Max's Kansas City and that was it! That was home. I just loved New York. Forget about Hollywood, this was where the chic intellectual junkie types hung out and I wanted to be one of them. I finally found a place where I felt I fit in and I never wanted to leave.

Back in L.A., I hooked up with a guy named Steven Hill, who played bass in a band called Lollipop, and in December we drove out to Chicago together, me and him and his band in an old Lincoln. I went home for a little while first, but my intention was to move to New York. I remember we arrived in a snowstorm, it was *so* cold. A few days later I flew to Orlando to spend Christmas with my mother.

Over the next few months is when I first started exotic dancing, at the Roman House in Chicago. My plan was to get some money together, ditch the boyfriend and move to New York with one of the other dancers. But right before we were going to leave, we got into a car accident on the way to the Roman House and she broke her arm, so she couldn't go with me. So I ended up going with Elida Ramirez, this crazy Mexican girl who had been following me around in L.A. and followed me to Chicago, and then a bunch of my girlfriends from Chicago came right after—Irma Ruiz, Jane, and Rock Out Claudette—all pro groupies. One of them needed an abortion, so they all came out with her. This would have been summer 1974. I was 17. We hit Club 82 the first night we got there [*famous old-time drag club turned glam rock venue, 82 East 4th St.*]. It was great!

Right away I started meeting all these people. I met Anya Phillips that first night at Club 82 and we started hanging out from that time [2].

She quickly became my best friend, traveling companion, confidante, muse—or was I her muse? We learned from each other. Anya and I became a pair, we went everywhere together. I loved her and she loved me! She had just moved from Hawaii and was living in midtown. I met like all my best friends in that first week or so. I knew a lot of girls, which was cool—I haven't spent much time with women since then, except when I was in prison, ha ha ha.

That first few weeks in New York was a whirlwind of bands, parties and sexual escapades. I hung out with Frenchy on St. Mark's Place, shopping in the thrift stores for monkey fur and old army jackets and fabulous '50s and '60s clothing. I got to know the manager of Club 82, Tommy, who was rumored to be a female-to-male sex change. And of course we went to Max's every night, and afterwards to Harold's Loft across the street. I loved walking into Harold's with some rock star and seeing other girls look jealously on. I was a big groupie! I fucked Jimmy Page and Jeff Beck—old school but big bucks. Jeff could suck his own dick. I liked that.

I loved everything about New York. Of course, Manhattan was very different back then. In the 1970s, because the crime was so bad and the city was kind of dilapidated, people didn't really want to live there, so rents were cheap. And there were a lot of different places you could go, like residential hotels, that don't exist anymore. Places like the Irving Hotel, where you could live inexpensively if you had just come to town or you were in between apartments. I moved around a lot the first couple of years I was in New York, but the first place I stayed was this little hotel at 79 Washington Place, the Village Plaza Hotel. It was a dive.

The Village Plaza, 79 Washington Place, has no doorman. A flaking sign by the tiny reception desk announces "Television

for Rental" amidst a forest of other signs;
"No Refunds," "All, Rents Must be Paid
in Advance," "No Checks Cashed," "No
Outgoing Calls for Transients."... The
elevator was out of order. The stairs were
dark and narrow, heavy with the sweet reek
of marijuana. A knock, and the door to [a
room] swung open. ... Against one of the
light green walls was a peeling gray dresser,
with the upper left drawer missing. ... Red
plastic flowers hung from an overhead light
fixture. The bathroom, directly across the
hall, was shared with other rooms.

—*The New York Times*

Arthur Kane lived down the hall. I had hung out with Arthur when
the Dolls came to Los Angeles and he might have mentioned that he
lived there, so that's why I went there. Arthur would sneak over to my
room to see me and he was always scared that Connie was going to
find out where he was. I had heard stories about her, how she was crazy
jealous and packed a knife, and I did not want any trouble with her.
Although I had a tough-girl exterior, inside I was not a fighter. Connie
and I did become friendly later on.

After a few weeks Elida and I rented an apartment, this really shitty
fifth-floor walkup on 76th Street between First and York. That building
should have been condemned. The apartment was sort of lopsided, it
sunk in at the center but it was only $75 a month, ridiculously cheap even
for those days. That's how it was in New York back then. Unbelievable,
right? Like when Johnny and I moved into our first apartment together,
it was $305 a month! Brand new building in Manhattan and it was three
hundred dollars.

Anyway, that place was so bad that I would sometimes stay with another friend on West 67th Street. She had a nice apartment she shared with Denise LaPiece, a stripper from Hell's Kitchen who hung out with the Harlots of 42nd Street [*early New York glitter band*], so that's how I met them. A lot of people from the symphony lived in that building, too.

And there was this Italian drug dealer, Luigi Ruggiero, who was around, too. He was hopelessly in love with me and submissive—the only sexual contact we had was when I allowed him to make love only to my feet, after I had been dancing all night! He followed me around like a homesick puppy. He was a Libra like me and I loved his humor and intellect. We became very close, he even lived with Elida and me for a little while. He used to take me to his sister's place in Queens for dinner. She grew her own vegetables in her backyard and made wine in the basement, and she would make us the most delicious home-cooked real Italian food I've ever had.

But things weren't going well with Elida, she started getting violent. She used to call me Cyndi Sleaze and she would hit me. Finally, Anya Phillips told me to get out of there and move in with her, so one day while Elida was at work I moved all my stuff out and Anya and I went to One Fifth Avenue. Which was like a hotel, but it was apartments—nice places, studios, one bedrooms—we had one of each [3]. I had my Hofner bass and my sewing machine, which Anya made great use of. We loved it there. Did a lot of acid, ha ha ha!

I don't know exactly what brought Anya to New York. She was born in Taiwan to a Taiwanese mother and an American father, and she had moved to Hawaii with some boyfriend, but I think her father was from back east and she probably always wanted to live there. She wanted to be a fashion designer, she was interested in clothing. We both wanted to make clothing. Anya had great designs—Debbie Harry wore a dress that she made on the cover of *Plastic Letters* [*Blondie's second album, released 1978*]. She came up with a lot of the outfits we wore, too. We used to dress in themes together, like cowgirls or sailors, we were really cute. I was the one who taught her to dress S&M and that had a big influence on her, she really liked that look and did a lot with it. When I first met Anya, she was wearing a pink bias-cut disco dress and had a shag haircut! She loved wearing pink, but after we started hanging out she switched from disco dresses to leather and rubber catsuits and short hair. We discovered Frankie and Marianne's store Ian's, which we loved—all the sex and fetish clothes! I bought my first vinyl and rubber shirts and skirts there, added them to my fantastic wardrobe which included wigs, hats, boots, bustiers and corsets. My favorite colors at the time were black and red, and a typical outfit would have been a black satiny mini-skirt, black corset, silk stockings, garters and Fredericks of Hollywood black knee-high stiletto boots, with a black velvet cape, red lipstick, red nail polish, false eyelashes, and a rhinestone choker. I had bright red hair and I liked to wear black berets, tilted Parisian style.

Anya was the type of woman I liked hanging out with—beautiful and bright. She had no fear. She was a ball of energy, very creative, very intelligent woman, and that's why I loved her. She really worshipped and loved me, too, and tried to be like me. She would even use my phrases and mannerisms. That was OK. She was beautiful, talented and intelligent, and a true punk.

> *Anya was brilliant, and way ahead of her time. She had more to do with punk's style than she is given credit for. I remember that Anya and Roxy were the first girls with Crazy Color hair, which they had gotten on a trip to London. — Eileen Polk*

Anya and I lived at One Fifth Avenue for a few months, then we decided to move to London. We had a lot of connections there and it seemed like the place to be. But London in the summer of 1975 was actually sort of boring. Glam was dying out and punk didn't exist yet. Really, there wasn't much of a scene at all, and when we got there, it turned out everything was happening in New York. But we hung out with Mott the Hoople and Gary Glitter and his band and some glam-type bands we had met in New York. I remember waking up with one of the guys from Gary Glitter's band at his house, and calling Anya and asking, "What's his name?" We also had the home phone numbers of some British guys I had been dating in New York, and Anya would call and tell their parents that she was here with their son's girlfriend Roxy from the U.S. and could we come over and stay at their place while we were in England? We went to several apartments and these women would just allow us to come in and take over, eating their food and leaving Crazy Color hair dye in their tubs!

Every day was hijinks and shenanigans. Like being wasted on Guinness and hash, trying to help Mott the Hoople pick out the single for their new album. Every song they would play for us, we'd go, "That's it! That's one!" We got in a lot of trouble, too: Anya was arrested for hash and put in Holloway prison and I had to go get her released. Ha! We were so high all the time we were there. We didn't care, we'd do anything for fun. It was magical.

We also hung out at Malcolm McLaren and Vivienne Westwood's SEX shop, in fact the first thing we did was go to SEX because we knew Malcolm from the New York Dolls. Malcolm and Sylvain Sylvain used to come over to One Fifth Avenue and visit us late at night, in a station wagon filled with clothing from his shops, and he would give us presents of clothes and stuff. I remember this one shirt I got from Malcolm, it said "Rock" in bones on the front, had tire treads on the sleeves and monkey hair coming out of the armpits. I loved it. [4] Then Anya would leave with Sylvain, I guess to have some fun, and they would leave Malcolm with me and we'd stay up and talk all night about England. I found it fascinating.

Malcolm McLaren, who became famous the following year as manager of the Sex Pistols, took charge of the New York Dolls in January 1975, although without a formal management contract. His brief run is generally credited with putting the last nail in the Dolls' coffin, as he attempted to combine their glam hedonism with radical left political symbols and Soviet-red vinyl outfits designed by his partner, Vivienne Westwood. After a series of shows in Florida in March, guitarist Johnny Thunders and drummer Jerry Nolan quit the band (final show: Dante's Den in Stuart, Florida, on March 31) and the Dolls effectively ended. Singer David Johansen returned promptly to New York; Thunders and Nolan followed and formed The Heartbreakers with Richard Hell and Walter Lure. Arthur Kane went to Los Angeles for a time, where he started Killer Kane with Blackie Lawless, later of the metal band W.A.S.P. Sylvain and McLaren road-tripped back to New York together in April. McLaren returned to London in May, but his influence on rock was just beginning. Captivated by the style of the New York underground, especially soon-to-be punk icon Richard Hell, McLaren and Westwood re-fashioned their Kings Road vintage clothing store Let It Rock into the

infamous bondage/fetish shop SEX. It was at
SEX in August or September 1975 that Johnny
Rotten auditioned for the band that became the
Sex Pistols, by gooning along with Alice Cooper's
"Eighteen" on the store's jukebox.

Before the Dolls, Sylvain Sylvain (Mizrahi) had
also run a used-clothing business out of his home
in Queens, New York.

*Malcolm was like some sort of labour holdover.
It was a Labour Party, power-to-the-people type
thing, but you couldn't meet a more capitalist
motherfucker in your life. Nonetheless, he
loved the idea of Communism. He liked the
posters and the graphic realism of the socialist
movement. He liked the surface of communism
but God forbid you should try to get a buck out
of him.  — Peter Jordan*

I liked Malcolm. We were friends. He was very interesting, he was
intelligent and very nice, and I had a crush on him at the time! Later,
when I got with Johnny, he was jealous of Malcolm. Johnny started a
fight with him once, when the Ramones played the Whisky with Blondie
[*February 16–20, 1977*]. That was the night Phil Spector came. Malcolm
came in and Johnny said to me, "Don't talk to him, don't even talk to
him, don't say hello." Johnny hated the Sex Pistols and he hated my

friendship with Malcolm. So I was scared, I didn't know what to do. Malcolm came over and sat next to me on the couch and put his arm around me, "Hey, how you been?" And I didn't answer him, because Johnny told me specifically not to say anything.

So he was like, "What's the matter with you?" And then: "Oh, is there a problem with your *boyfriend?*" and that's all Johnny needed. Then I think Malcolm said something stupid like, "You wanna step outside?" Ha ha ha! The next thing, Johnny had a chair over his head, ready to bash him, and everybody was like, "Whoa!" Malcolm fled. I was embarrassed, but I liked the attention and knowing that Johnny would fight for me. I've always loved men who could fight.

Johnny was very violent—that's what I liked about him. I like guys like that, I've married quite a few. That was the submissive time. I was totally submissive to Johnny the whole time we lived together. Wherever he went, I went. What he wanted to do, we did. He tried to change me and I went along with it, to the point that my friends didn't even recognize me anymore. He told me what to wear, who I could talk to, where I could stand, what I could drink—everything. Everything.

But when I first met him I was *insane*, you know? I was running around in bondage clothing and Fredericks of Hollywood corsets and panties and little leather skirts and stuff like that. I had tons of makeup and Crazy Color in my hair, really wild, and that's what he was attracted to me for, I thought. But eventually he wanted to change all that. He didn't like that I knew everybody on the scene and everybody knew me. We would be walking down the street and people would yell, "Hey, Roxy!" at me and not look twice at him. He hated that. That's what caused a lot of our fights—our going out and running into ex-boyfriends of mine.

⌘

I was an exotic dancer in New York from the time I moved there at age 17 until I started living with Johnny when I was 20. Most dancers don't go by their real names, they have stage names, and I always liked the name Roxanne so I started calling myself Roxy.

*She took her name because she loved Roxy Music! We used to get loaded on speed and listen to Roxy Music for days. Someone should remind her of that. — Gyda Gash*

I remember there were three of us who went to audition together, me and Anya and somebody else. There used to be an agency that booked all the girls into different clubs, what was his name—Milton. He called himself Mambo [5]. He was on 57th Street, and we'd go up there once a week and get booked. I got him a little present once, remember when everybody was wearing those gold-plated or silver-plated razor blade necklaces? I bought him one of those and then we went out for drinks that night and got really plastered.

Anya and I worked at different clubs every night, mostly on Long Island. It paid $17 an hour back then, minus an agent fee of 10%—couldn't beat that. We had so much fun. You'd see us all on the Long Island Railroad, drunk in the bar car, on our way to Port Washington and other exotic stations. It was a perfect job for me. We did blotter acid at work, customers would buy you drinks all day and night, and I always had my supply of black beauties (*Biphetamine, a combined amphetamine that came in a black capsule*) and Tuinals (*a powerful*

*sedative containing two different barbiturates*)—those and Colt 45 kept
me going! I'd run out at 6:00 a.m. in an Ian's flasher trench coat, corset,
stockings, stilletto boots and make-up from the night before to get my
Colt 45. I woke up with a Colt and a black beauty, and I fell asleep with
a Colt and a Tuinal. I used to buy my pills from this Viet Nam veteran
who got them from the VA. There was such a variety, so many fun pills!
Like Quaaludes. I bought white crosses (*Dexedrine*) and Seconal by the
bottle full. There were no rehabs—no one *wanted* to straighten up and
get sober!

I did a lot of amphetamines, so I had a lot of energy and could go for
long periods without any sleep. I would do double shifts, dance for like
16, 18 hours a day. At that time everybody was doing heroin, but I never
really liked it; I was in the small minority of people who liked speed
instead of heroin. I used to live off of black beauties and speed, so I made
a lot of money! We all made a lot of money, you know—Gyda [*Gash*],
Nancy [*Spungen*], all the girls. Everybody.

I had plenty of money. Besides what I made, my mother would send
money every week, which I wouldn't touch. I wanted to show her I could
take care of myself. I don't know what she thought I was doing there, but
as long as I stayed away she was relieved and would send money.

Yeah, back then the girls had all the money. We were all exotic
dancers who took care of the musicians before they were established,
hoping they would make it big. We would take turns fucking different
musicians from the local bands. I had to have a different one every night,
what a slut! It was quantity, not quality back then. But we were all one
big happy family, and we interchanged guys and boyfriends all the time.
We were sluts, we were groupies, we were drug addicts, we passed
around boyfriends and then compared notes and talked and laughed
about how they were in bed, ha!

*It was a very free time, where we'd dance,*
*make a shitload of money, drink all day, 'cause*
*people would buy you drinks or whatever—we'd*
*go to the clubs and then we'd wind up in bed*
*with some guy. It was always some guy in some*
*band, and that was every night. Every night.*
*Always going out.*  — *Gyda Gash*


I was at Max's Kansas City every night. Even if I was dancing on Long Island and could only get there for five minutes before they closed, I would do it. I didn't care, I had to be out. Sometimes Anya ("The Peking Doll") and I would go to our boss's house after dancing and earn some extra money putting on shows—we had an S&M thing, with her domme and me playing sub—and then we would take a taxi all the way back to the city, no matter how late it was. We had to be seen every night! We lived for the clubs.

Max's was great. Everybody went there. We knew everybody, everybody knew each other, it was like a big family, you know? I even lived near Max's for a little while, at the Irving Hotel. [*Max's Kansas City was at 213 Park Avenue South; the Irving Hotel was a few blocks away, at 26 Gramercy Park South.*] I was living there with Marc Bell [*drummer with the Voidoids, later Marky Ramone*] when I started seeing Johnny Ramone. Gyda lived there before me, then she and Cheetah [*Chrome, guitarist with the Dead Boys*] lived there after they got together. I introduced them. I had met Cheetah first, but we didn't fuck because he had the clap and was being gallant. But I thought he'd look cute with Gyda, and it sounded good—Gyda and Cheetah [6].

After the original Max's closed down [*December 1974*] [7], people were like, Where the fuck do you go? We didn't know what to do anymore, where's anybody go, where are you gonna be tonight, you know? This was right before everybody started hanging out at CBGB. So that winter, 1975, everybody was hanging out at Ashley's, which was right across the street from where Anya and I lived. All of a sudden we were chairing a lot of backgammon games there, ha ha ha! We would go every night and order paté and bottles of Pouilly-Fouissé. I don't know what the hell we were trying to be!

Ashley's was higher class or something, they were sort of snobby but it was fun. Downstairs was a fancy restaurant, and then you went up the staircase and there was a bar. I never went to Studio 54 ever, I wouldn't go there because I was totally against that type of people, but I think it might have been sort of like a Studio 54-type of crowd. It was sort of disco-y but they played good music, and the old crowd from Max's all started going there. Anya and I were there every single night.

*Ashley's was a fancy rock star celebrity club. All the English bands went there. I saw John Lennon there one night. It had an upstairs and a downstairs bar but no dance floor, always crowded. — Eileen Polk*

I met a few people at Ashley's, like Richard Rockwood. Right before I started hanging out with musicians, I went through this phase of wanting a boyfriend who was an artist, and English, so I found Richard. He was an artist, British, did a drawing of me for a magazine. Later Anya decided I wasn't good for Richard, so she grabbed him and moved him in with her, because she was trying to hang out with a lot of arty-farty types at that time.

In the end, though, Ashley's wasn't the same as Max's, and I guess that's why we decided to go to London. I sold my Hofner bass, we got rid of everything and went to England, must have been May or June. As soon as we got there, everything started happening in New York. I kept reading about all the bands in New York and what was going on there, all our friends! So we didn't stay long in England, only a couple of months, I think. Once we saw all the papers writing about New York, we came back.

**CBGB's Festival of Unsigned Bands took place in July 1975 and helped bring the underground music scene to wider attention. The Festival was written up in *Rolling Stone* and the UK music magazine *Melody Maker*, possibly among the press reports that prompted Roxy and Anya to return quickly to New York.**

When we came back we had no place to live, so we went to One Fifth Avenue again for a while, then we stayed with the fat drummer from the Harlots of 42nd Street, Tony [*D'Ambra*]. That was a mistake! He got weird and wanted us to fuck him for letting us stay there—when we didn't, he threw us out. Then we went and stayed with Eliot, Eliot Kidd Cohen. Walter Lure [*guitarist, later with the Heartbreakers*] was living there, too. And we stayed with Richard Rockwood, but everyone was telling him to stay away from me, that I was bad for him. Richard tended to get a little out of control when I was around and drink too much, so people didn't like him being around me. Always happens! Story of my life.

*I found a 'Chicago' postcard from Anya dated August 19, 1975. Anya writes: 'I hate this lousey city' and 'Roxy has been in the mental hospital (thanks to her mother) but got out today.' I think Anya was one of the few people who actually met Roxy's mother.  — Eileen Polk*

Yeah, well, Anya and I were doing a lot of blotter acid, ha ha ha! Blotter acid was going around and my old boyfriend Luigi got a shipment of it. It seemed like everybody was on this blotter acid for a while. We were tripping one day and Anya just sort of freaked out, she was panicking, so I took her to Chinatown and it calmed her down. She thought she was back in Taiwan or something! But then we started looking at the streets and: "Oh, it's so *dirty* here! We gotta get *out* of here!"

So we took a cab to the airport and flew to Chicago. When we got there we went on a shopping spree on my mother's credit cards, bought thousands of dollars worth of clothes, and then proceeded to drink everything in my mother's liquor cabinet! So my mother took me across the street to a psychiatric hospital and checked me in, and she put Anya in a motel downtown somewhere far away from her place. Five days later, after observation, I finally got out of the psych ward, found Anya, and we escaped to Peoria to see Sparks, then back to New York for the Sparks party at Burger King. And then a week or two later, we went to the Ramones show where I met Johnny.

He and I didn't have any kind of a relationship at first—he didn't have my number, and I didn't see him again for a while after that show. But I remembered him, and he remembered me, too.

⌘

By the Fall of '75 things with Anya were changing, and I was pretty angry with her. She would stay home to sew while I worked, she was supposedly making clothes, our designs, but she'd run over to Richard Hell's (or Dickie Heck, as she called him) and buy dope with the money I would leave her for supplies. I got sick of her letting me down when I was working so hard.

> *By the time I met Roxy, Anya was tired of her as a roommate. Roxy drank a lot, and Anya didn't drink as much, so that was the problem. Anya did not do well with any roommate she could badger because she was so sadistic. You had to be strong and defend your turf to live with Anya! She would attack any weakness.*
> *— Eileen Polk*

One day I was in Mamoun's Falafel on MacDougal Street—I was friends with Mamoun, so I was in there a lot—and he had a sign up that said there was an apartment for rent right across the street, 128 MacDougal, so I went to look at it and immediately rented it. That was pretty much it for me and Anya as roommates. She moved back in with me a few weeks later, but it didn't last long.

Richard Rockwood was still my boyfriend when I lived on MacDougal. So was Brian Brain, another English artist, and Luigi was still around, too. Brian lived across the street from me on MacDougal. Eliott used to call that place "Roxy's United Nations."

*I don't remember that Anya and Roxy had a 'falling out' but I'm sure by Christmas of '75, Anya was moving on to other things. At that time she was living with me at my mother's house in the West Village. She was going to set up some kind of business, but she ended up having a punk rock 'salon' there instead! We had all the bands come over to beautiful dinners that Anya would cook. She would entertain in her pink negligees!*

*I also remember Brian Brain was in love with Roxy because one night, whatever 'getaway car' Dee Dee had arranged for he and I to escape from Connie also contained Johnny and Roxy, and Brian Brain threw himself on the hood of the car crying and screaming. This was typical of punk nights, and I recall Connie used the same technique. So perhaps Brian learned it from Connie! Maybe Brian Brain was just a short fling for Roxy, or maybe he was in love with her and she didn't care, but the memory is burned into my mind because it was so dramatic. Brian was very smart, and English, but not a cute punk rock star—he was a bit older than us. He was a good artist and did a lot of flyers for bands. He struck me as a college professor who had dropped out. I really don't know what was between him and Roxy, but he was quite upset when she met Johnny.*

*— Eileen Polk*

*There were these two guys, an Italian guy named Luigi—he's dead and gone—and a British guy named Brian Brain. Completely crazy speed freaks, older guys, way older than us. ... I know Luigi was a speed dealer. They were real characters, I mean, straight out of Zap comics, confirmed freaks, drugs, out of their minds — and she loved them, because the more crazy the person, the more she loved them. And she was hanging out with Marc Bell for a long time and I don't know, various cast of characters. She had a girlfriend too, a groupie from Chicago, black chick, really cute, really hot and sexy, her name was LaMumba—it was great! All kinds of freaks. — Gyda Gash*

# 1976

JOHNNY RAMONE WASN'T in the picture yet, but he was around and funny enough, Anya liked him, too. While she was staying with me at MacDougal Street, she saw him at Max's one night and gave him some monsters, some Japanese robots. He drove her back that night, hoping to see me. He asked her, "Where's your red-headed friend?" and she told him I wasn't there—told him I had moved back to Chicago, when actually I was right inside! Ha ha ha! Because *she* liked him!

But Anya was too fat for Johnny. He liked a particular kind of woman, he liked sexy, big-breasted women. Like Tura Satana. *Ilsa, She-Wolf of the SS*—Dyanne Thorne. Caroline Munro. Jane Fonda in *Barbarella.*

Yeah, she told him I didn't live there anymore and that I'd gone back to Chicago. He later ended up giving those robots to me.

*Anya would always flirt with every cute guy in a band, but she would never have been that interested in any of the Ramones — too dumb or too right-wing for her. Anya was one of the smartest people I knew. She was also a world traveler, while a lot of the groupies were just in from the boondocks and didn't know anything. Anya was the first anarchist I ever met, and she was a great influence on me. I would never let her dominate me, which is why we stopped living together. But she is one of the most important people in my life and I loved her very much. Anya had a Svengali effect on anyone who associated closely with her — she was such a strong personality that she changed everyone she came in contact with. Her philosophy of life was the exact opposite from the dumb guy 'hamburgers and cruising for girls and beer' mentality of the Punk magazine gang, although she could appreciate the fun aspect of this stuff. She was much more interested in Richard Hell, Television, Talking Heads, Lydia Lunch, poetry and literature. She was a well-read intellectual, spoke fluent Mandarin and Cantonese Chinese, knew all about the Situationists and other anarchist groups, Paris May 1968, etc. The great contradiction was that Anya was an anarchist, but she LOVED money and nice clothes. She loved Other People's Money! — Eileen Polk*

Anya really "broke up" with me over Nancy Spungen one night. It was Nancy's birthday [*February 27, 1976*] and she and I were going out to dinner together. Anya stopped over and saw me with Nancy and she got so upset, she took all her stuff and left in a rage. Anya was very jealous. She didn't like me hanging out with anybody else and when she saw Nancy there, she just flipped out. She was so mad that I was doing something without her, with another girl who she didn't particularly like, that she moved out. I didn't see her after that for a long time. The next time I saw her, she was with James Chance.

*Anya was hostile to many people and her hostilities changed constantly. She thrived on anger and seemed to need someone to be mad at at all times. Usually it was NOT her famous friends, only her buddies and fellow punks, so that pissed a lot of people off.* — Eileen Polk

I knew Nancy Spungen from Max's. She had just moved from Philadelphia to New York, to be around the bands, I guess. She didn't know what to do with herself. I remember she wanted a job, she wanted to do what the other girls did—be an exotic dancer. She was pretty young, like 16, I think. I was a year or two older than her. She was underage, like all of us, but we got her into dancing and I would hang out with her sometimes. She had a nice apartment that her parents paid for. Compared to everybody else, she had a really nice apartment, with furniture! I liked going over there once in a while to sleep in a bed. Everything was nice and clean.

Nancy was like a little old Jewish woman when she woke up in the morning, with her curlers in her hair and her bathrobe. Always complaining, and nobody really liked her, she had a bad attitude. She wasn't a real nice person, but she took in a lot of band members and let them stay with her, various guys who didn't have a place to stay. I guess she was looking for a boyfriend or something.

I remember we talked about going to England, I thought maybe the two of us could go together. But then I got involved with Johnny, so she ended up going first [*in December 1976 or January 1977, following Jerry Nolan, drummer for the Heartbreakers*] and then she got together with Sid [*Vicious*]. That was right before Johnny and I started living together. [*Sid and Nancy became a couple in February 1977, at the same time Glen Matlock quit the Sex Pistols and Sid joined the band.*]

I was friendly with her. Everybody thinks she was horrible—she *was* horrible. But I sort of felt bad for Nancy because the guys I knew would go over and stay at her place and take her food, take her drugs, and then make fun of her behind her back. They'd use her. I know Dee Dee Ramone was over there sleepin' once in a while, he told me.

We saw her in London at a party after the Ramones played [*June 5 or 6, 1977*]. She was talking with an English accent and dragging Sid around with her, introducing him to everyone. They were both high and making a spectacle of themselves. Sid didn't have much to say—hullo was about it. But Johnny didn't like her, he didn't like Nancy at all because she was on drugs and a bitch. I remember when she died, he came in and tossed the newspapers: "No more Nancy!"

⌘

Soon after the thing with Anya and Nancy, I left MacDougal Street and Eliot Kidd ended up with that apartment. He was a big drug dealer, he went to prison for drug-dealing years later. He had a band, too, the Demons—Walter Lure was in his band before he was in the Heartbreakers. Remember the Demons? Horrible album, but they were a lot of fun to hang out with! I loved Eliot. We had such fun together.

I met him at Harold's Loft, where a lot of characters used to hang

out [*210 Fifth Avenue at 26th St.*]. That place was great! It was open all
night. I remember it was Thanksgiving. He followed me around for a
while, then he grabbed my purse and started kicking it down the hall and
into the elevator. I ran up and he threw me into the elevator! Downstairs,
Walter Lure was waiting in his car with the rest of the band. Eliot threw
me in the backseat and we took off to his place in Brooklyn. It was
exciting, fun and scary—I liked that combination. I had some blotter
acid, he had champagne, we tripped and played B&D games all day and
the next day. He tied me up and used the champagne bottle on me, and
we watched "The Wizard of Oz" and laughed our heads off. He was
such fun. It turned out we had the same birthday, October 4, and he told
me wherever he was on his birthday, he would always remember me.
Strangely enough, he died on his birthday in 1998, after his body rejected
a liver transplant.

Anya and I brought a lot of celebrities to Harold's—the Gary Glitter
Band, Jeff Beck, all the visiting British bands. Johnny Thunders was
always there, too. I was drawn to him, he always seemed so sad. He was
missing Sable Starr, who he had met in L.A. on the Dolls' first tour, same
time as I met them. I guess she and Johnny pretty much fell in love at
first sight and she moved to New York to be with him, but left him over
the drugs. So he was out and about a lot. Black Tony the drug dealer was
the procurer for Johnny Thunders' little get-togethers. He worked at The
Late Show, next to where Trash & Vaudeville is now. Frenchy ran that
place—what a doll! We bought a lot of clothes there. [*The Late Show, at
2 St. Mark's Place, was a used/vintage clothing store owned by Christian
"Frenchy" Rodriguez, who had also served as roadie and wardrobe
manager for the New York Dolls.*] After Harold's, Tony would invite a
few girls for a private party at Johnny's and provide the drugs—speed,
heroin. I would always try to resist and play hard to get, but I was curious
about Johnny.

After Eliot took over my MacDougal St. apartment I didn't have a place to live. I was sort of a rolling stone at that point, still working all the time and staying mainly in hotels like the George Washington or the Gramercy Park. Then my sister Carolyn came to New York to visit. She used to come out every year for like a week and stay at the St. Moritz, so when she came to town I just went and stayed there with her! Of course.

This particular visit was when I started hanging around with Marc Bell, of Richard Hell's Voidoids and Wayne County fame. He had gotten stabbed, he was in the hospital, and I got in touch with him. I told him I was at the St. Moritz, and the next thing I knew he left the hospital and showed up at the St. Moritz in his hospital gown and bandages for free drinks and room service, ha ha ha! We spent days in the bar, going to Max's every night, dressing Carolyn in my clothes. Then I guess he moved in with me, wherever I was going he was going, too. But all we did was drink. And—drink. And go crazy.

Before I met Marc, I used to screw his twin brother once in a while, Fred Bell, who was rather handsome. That's how I got to know Marc. Fred was a lot more fun, but I liked Marc better because he was an established musician. I think Marc liked me at least partly because he had an insane foot fetish. He had a lot of fetishes back then, like skirts, and high-heeled shoes, which he liked to suck on at the bar at Max's. And we both loved to drink and I needed a partner. He was a big drunk then—of course, so was everyone else! Everyone drank and/or was a big drunk, Eileen Polk, Legs McNeil, Lester Bangs, Joey Ramone, Anya, Gyda, we all drank. It was strange for me *not* to drink. I didn't know any other way to live, and it made it easier for me to be me and talk to all these people who were famous.

Yeah, those two brothers, Fred and Marc, ha! They were pretty funny. They were both, like, happy drunks. They would fight a lot, but they were cute.

Marc's girlfriend Amy was a friend of mine, too. She had gone out west and was having his baby in Phoenix, so I got together with

Marc and we moved into the Irving Hotel. We had sex, but we were really more like drinking buddies. Other than that it wasn't exactly a great match, in fact we had very little in common. For one thing, Marc was always hungry and food made me sick, so that was always a bone of contention between us. His sidekick Elwood from Chicago used to complain that I never fed him. Well, that was not my department, not my job. After the Irving, we moved to a storefront in Soho, on Thompson St., and I remember Marc going out around the neighborhood and stealing huge cans of food—I guess they were for restaurants—he would steal these tremendous cans of food and then sit and eat out of them! And he always seemed to have some flunky around, some minion doing his bidding, like Elwood, who I knew from Chicago, or Stinkfoot, who came on tour with us once.

⌘

Then one night I ran into Johnny Ramone at Max's. He was alone that night and he said he'd been looking for me. I was high and I grabbed him and dragged him out to his little Chevy Vega, which was parked right across the street, and fucked him. It was *greeeaaaat!* Ha ha! It was wild. In the back seat of his Vega across the street from Max's Kansas City!—I just dragged him out and we did it.

*I remember the night they met at Max's and I
could tell Johnny was completely smitten. He*

*was fascinated with her. I think Johnny was*
*married at the time so they kept the affair*
*quiet for awhile, but by the summer of '76, they*
*were definitely a couple. — Eileen Polk*

Johnny drove me home that night and asked for my phone number. At the time I was living with Marc at the Irving Hotel. A few days later he called me; he said, "This is John." I said, "John who?" I only knew him as Johnny, but he liked being called John.

"You know, John. I met you the other night. I have the red Vega."

"Oh, Johnny! Hi, how ya doin'? What's up, I was just getting ready to go to work."

"Oh, I was hoping you were free to go to dinner with me." Was he asking me out on a *date?*

A little while later, he picked me up. It was one of the only dates I ever went on in my life. We went to Little Italy, to Luna's [*old-school Italian restaurant at 115 Mulberry St.*]. And we talked. Here was a man who was actually interested in me, talking to me, listening to my opinions, my life. He wasn't just interested in fucking me. After dinner, he drove me to work, wherever I was dancing that night. But he wouldn't come in—told me he didn't want to see me like that, even though he'd already fucked me in the back seat of his car! I thought that was sweet.

This would have been March or maybe early April of 1976. I know I started seeing him right around the time the Ramones first album came out [Ramones *was released April 23, 1976*] because I carried that album with me everywhere and made everyone listen to it!

From then on, we pretty much saw each other all the time. We had to sneak around at first because we both lived with someone else. But by July, when the Ramones went to England, John and I were definitely

together. I remember because Eileen Polk and I went out to meet Johnny
and Dee Dee at the airport when they came back from England—we
rented a limo for them.

In July 1976, the Ramones went to London for
the first time. They played only two dates, the
Roundhouse on July 4 and Dingwalls on July 5,
but these shows were a major catalyst for the
punk movement. It is not true that the Ramones
"started punk" when they went to England;
the scene was already underway in both New
York and London. The Sex Pistols had been
performing since the previous November, the
London punk look (partly inspired by Richard
Hell via Malcolm McLaren's SEX shop, but also
created by the Pistols' fans themselves) was
established, and many of the first-wave British
punk bands had formed. The Clash played their
first gig on July 4 in Sheffield, opening for the
Sex Pistols; both bands came out to see the
Ramones the next night; the Damned debuted
the following night, July 6 [1].

But it was the Ramones' powerful, coherent,
original sound and image—created with minimal
technique and no money—that galvanized the
young English fans and propelled what had been
essentially the Sex Pistols' following into a new
musical and artistic movement. Overnight, punk
became the voice of full-on revolution against
the older, established "rock aristocracy"—the

Rolling Stones, The Who, Yes, Pink Floyd, Led
Zeppelin, etc.—and the music business itself.
The controversy and excitement generated by
the British punk bands quickly rebounded to the
U.S., inspiring not only an enormous number of
new bands but an entire alternative/DIY music
and art scene all across the country from the
mid-'70s through the 1980s. Much of the credit
for the wide dispersal of punk in the U.S. goes
directly to the Ramones, who were willing to play
small towns and venues as well as major ones.

Despite its influence, the full impact of punk
was slow to appear in mainstream American
rock, mostly due to intense resistance from the
music industry. It was not until Nirvana and the
grunge movement of the early 1990s that punk
finally registered above ground, and the bands
who helped create it—especially the Ramones—
started getting their due. By then, of course, the
Ramones were at the end of their 22-year career.

Yeah, when Johnny went to England, we were already boyfriend and
girlfriend. That's why I went out to pick him up, I wouldn't normally go
out of my way to pick somebody up at the airport. Eileen was seeing Dee
Dee at the time and she wanted to get a limo—I was sort of embarrassed,
I didn't think it was necessary. They didn't seem like the same sort of
rock stars as the ones before them, they didn't want a limousine. But it
was fun, we had a good time. I remember they were very excited about

what was going on over in England with all the bands starting up, all these kids who looked up to the Ramones and started new bands because of the Ramones.

*Roxy and I picked up Johnny and Dee Dee and we had a wonderful time, she had a big bottle of champagne waiting for them. This was in the summer of '76 and I remember that summer was the Bicentennial, when all the ships from all over the world were in NY Harbor and the city was full of sailors! After we picked up Johnny and Dee Dee at the airport, we came back to my mother's house and watched the movie* The Producers *on TV and laughed our asses off at "Springtime for Hitler!"* — Eileen Polk

Johnny was a real gentleman and fun and excited about things when I first met him. We went to a lot of movies, did all kinds of outdoor stuff...we had pretty wild sex back then. Like in the parks. Outside on the street, sitting on a motorcycle—he'd just pick me up and fuck me. I remember going to the park and laying on a blanket, kissing. I had on a corset and stockings, mini skirt and boots and no underwear! He loved it. Sometimes I asked him to wear his motorcycle jacket and I had bought him some motorcycle boots. But he couldn't wear them because he was extremely flat-footed and it hurt him to walk in them. He would have made a good cop—flat-foot, Irish, ha! Anyhow, he'd put them on to fuck me and I'd wear my frilly white underwear and ankle socks, or a corset and crotchless panties, depending on his mood. He liked getting head, too, and giving it. He was good at it. We had sex a lot. Too bad his herpes got so bad after awhile. I tried to get him to see a doctor—there was no reason for him to suffer. But he absolutely hated doctors, and being sick.

⌘

*I remember Johnny's girlfriend at the time wore a black rubber dress with armpit hair sewn onto it! ... [T]hey always had this whole vibe of leather, loudness, and extreme girls, in high heels and usually some kind of bondage dress, with bleached blonde hair done up really big! — Chris Frantz*

**Roxy**, *that* chick, repulsive as ever in outdated black mini vinyl gear and lopsided wig, still trying to win herself some unlucky loser's heart by her wanton ways seen on L.I. railroad giving conductors coronary attacks en route to see **Ramones** and **Fast** at My Father's Place... [*refers to show of July 13, 1976*]
　　　　—*New York Rocker*, "Pressed Lips"

*Roxy and I took the Long Island Railroad
train from Penn Station to go out to one of
those Ramones shows at My Father's Place.
It was during the Democratic Convention in
New York City [July 12–15, 1976] and we
were dressed up totally crazy and had to go
through the station during the convention
that took place upstairs in Madison Square
Garden. You can imagine Roxy and I in our
punk dominatrix gear had quite an interesting
effect on all those politicians!* — Eileen Polk

Marc knew I was seeing Johnny. He knew right away when Johnny
called me that day. I didn't know who it was and when I realized who it
was, I said to Marc, "Oh it's Johnny Ramone," or whatever. I didn't keep
it a secret or anything. But he wasn't too happy about it.

And Johnny didn't particularly like the Irving Hotel, he only stayed
there one night, I think. He told me to get an apartment, so I did. Soon
after our "first date," I moved out of the Irving and into a storefront on
Thompson Street between Houston and Prince, across from the Betsey
Johnson store [*which was at 130 Thompson St.*]. Marc came with me at
first, but I had already started seeing Johnny, and then Amy came back to
town and I didn't want any complications with her. Amy was a tough girl
and I was a little scared that she would want to beat me up. But when I
finally ran into her one night at Max's, she was cool. She had heard I was
hanging out with Marc and didn't mind at all, in fact, she needed a place
to stay and spent a night or two on Thompson St.

And Marc always had Marion [*Flynn*], too, Marion was hanging
around. I think he sort of tried to keep her hidden away, but she was

always around. I didn't even know she was his girlfriend, I thought
Amy was, but I guess Marion had always been his true love or whatever,
childhood sweetheart. He never showed any affection toward her. But
then, the only affection he ever showed toward me in public was licking
my stiletto heels! [*Marc Bell and Marion Flynn were married in 1984.*]
Anyway, I came home one day and his stuff was packed up.

So Marc left and I gave Johnny a key. That storefront was a great
place. Everyone stayed there! I loved it. Johnny hated it. He didn't like
that apartment. Not at all. He never lived there, he just came to see me
every day. He didn't want to move in there—too many bugs. I remember
chasing giant waterbugs around that storefront with the "Beat on the
Brat" baseball bats that were promotional items for the first album. Little
bats! Those things must be real collector's items now [2].

> Outside CBGB, Johnny, between sets
> one evening, said how much he enjoyed
> staying up all night with his wife
> watching late movies on TV. One of his
> favorites is "Now Voyager."
> —*New York Rocker*

> Well, **Roxy** seems to have won her man,
> John Cummings (alias Ramone), much
> to his lovely wife's chagrin...
> —*New York Rocker*, "Pressed Lips"

Johnny was still living in Queens with his wife, and he went
back and forth trying to figure out what he wanted to do. He was very

indecisive. He'd try to stay away, but he couldn't. He'd leave, but he was on a pay phone to me before he even got home, and then back at my place as soon as possible. Really, the problem was he was afraid to leave his wife because of what his parents would say. He felt guilty for leaving her, and he felt some sort of obligation to his mother to stay with her. I guess it was his Catholic upbringing, that he was supposed to stay married no matter what, but it didn't make any sense to me. I mean, his family hated her. *Hated* her. They did not like that he had married a Jewish woman. But she had big knockers and a big ego and liked to fuck, so what the hell. And her family hated him—Rosana's brothers actually beat him up on the day of their wedding! He told me they got into this big fight over something, I forget what it was, but they had this huge fight and they beat him up and threw him out of the house. This after he had been a good sport and gone along with the Jewish wedding, even worn a yarmulke! [3].

And yet he stayed married to her for quite some time, because even after we were together, the whole time we were living together and "engaged" or whatever, he still didn't get a divorce. Seven years! (*1977–83*) I used to say to him all the time, "I think you really should get divorced before you make some really good money and she takes it all! You've got to make some sort of a deal with her." But it seemed like he was happy to keep things going as they were. He didn't want his mother to be disappointed in him. Yeah, it took him seven years to divorce Rosana. She even used to cut his hair until I put my foot down and told him to find someone else! But finally they did divorce [4].

I didn't usually fuck around with married guys, nor guys that had girlfriends; that wasn't me. I wouldn't want it done to me. Maybe I should have seen a pattern, but it was such a short pattern at the time that I never thought about it. Plus we were so inseparable, so much in love. We talked about getting married, but back then I didn't really care about that. It wasn't necessary. I didn't think I ever would get married, I didn't really believe in the idea. I was for women's lib and found marriage archaic and man-made to trap a woman and ruin her. Marriage was for boring people, you know? Punk rockers didn't believe in marriage. I like getting married now, I've been married six times! And all my husbands spoke to Johnny. But back then I was a free spirit and a feminist. I also never had the craving for children to make myself whole or to find my identity. I thought there were enough people in the world. Johnny was an only child and never had to share anyone with anyone else, so he didn't want children either, and if I were going to have a child it would have been with him. He got me pregnant twice.

But in the beginning it was all very romantic and exciting. Once in a while he would devise these schemes where his wife would go out of town so I could come and stay at his place for the weekend. He'd be the perfect host, making drinks and ordering take-out. We'd watch a horror film and fuck. It was heaven for me, everything was nice and clean and new—not like my place, which at the time was more transient than homey.

Mostly, though, he came to my place. He would pick me up early in his Vega and we'd go out. He would call in the morning to say he was leaving, or call on the way to say he was almost there or looking for a parking space. That car finally broke down one day coming from Forest Hills, and he just left it on the bridge and took a taxi to me. When Marc was living there I would meet Johnny outside. After Marc left, Johnny got the key and he would just walk in on whatever was going on. I wouldn't get to sleep until 6 a.m. or so, and he'd leave Forest Hills as soon as Rosana left for work, so we'd go out early, shopping, restaurants, sight-seeing and to the movies. I wasn't getting much sleep! But we were really in love. He centered me and kept me focused on trying to be more normal during the day, instead of living like a vampire.

We had a lot of fun when we were first dating. He would pick me up and we'd find stuff to do all day. He couldn't wait to drag me to Coney Island to show me the sideshows and explain what a "geek" really was—a person who worked the sideshows, usually a drunk, who would bite the heads off chickens for alcohol. We played silly games, rode the bumper cars and the Cyclone, and went through the "Hell Hole," where the floor dropped out from under you. It was exhilarating! It was great fun. And I remember going to see a double-feature of *Mutations* and *Freaks* with him. He was so proud of taking me, since I had never seen these films before! Johnny was fascinated with freaks and geeks, he loved any sort of oddity or atrocity. He loved pinheads and wondered what had happened to them all, why we didn't see any freaks anymore. Because they're killed at birth, I told him. He also loved *Nightmare Alley*, this hideous, spellbinding film where Tyrone Power is reduced to a circus geek. He introduced me to old horror and science fiction I hadn't seen. I loved it, I've always loved horror, the unusual, the bizarre, anything different, anything kinky or rough. Then he'd have to leave in order to be home before his wife got home. He would go home around 5:00, I would go to work and then to Max's or Harold's Loft afterwards. And Johnny would come opening the door early the next morning and find people strewn all over and bounce everyone out.

**Connie Ramone**'s legs look more like bent toothpicks than ever after her successful attempts at dieting. Not Fade Away. Have she and Dee Dee had their final breakup? We'll see after the Ramones California return...

—*New York Rocker,* "Pressed Lips"

*There are so many terrible stories about Connie, but you know, she wasn't terrible, she had spark and life and passion and she was a lot of fun. The whole scene was kind of wild and she was, too. So much about those times doesn't translate that well to today, but I honestly don't think Arthur or Dee Dee would have wanted it any other way. Arthur probably wasn't amused about the whole thumb thing, but that's another story.   — Ann Henderling*

Connie Ramone, whose real name was Connie Gripp, also stayed at the storefront with me. She had nowhere to go and I said, "Well, you can put your things over here, you can stay here." She had all these costumes, lots of cool clothes, boxes and boxes of clothes that she brought over. I remember one day I wore some of her clothes when I went out to Queens to see Johnny. He had sent his wife to San Juan or something and he invited me over to his place in Forest Hills for piña coladas, and I wore Connie's clothes. She dressed like a rag doll. Maybe it was from when she used to hang out with the New York Dolls, but her clothes looked sort of like adult baby clothes, even though she was not a small person. Connie was tall and thin, with bleached blonde hair. She was cool-looking. And she was a great drinking partner. She was heartsick about Dee Dee and was an alcoholic like I was without my amphetamines [5].

*I heard Connie was from Fort Worth, Texas, and was abused (probably physically and sexually) as a child. I heard she came from a Christian fundamentalist family ... I even heard her father was a preacher. But this could also be myth. She moved to L.A., became a groupie [Connie had been friends with some members of Frank Zappa's teenage groupie contingent, the GTOs—Girls Together Outrageously—and adopted their sobriquet, calling herself Miss Connie for a while] and then moved to New York. She loved bass players! But I don't know much about her. I had a weird relationship with Connie, we would get into fistfights, duke it out, and then go for a drink and laugh about it! She was outrageous, would steal from people's purses in the clubs. But in a weird way I liked her. She even spent the night at my house once, and I thought she might stab me in my bed! But she was really nice sometimes. She had been so abused by men and abused them back. Connie was probably very mentally ill.*

— *Eileen Polk*

*Connie definitely had a temper and she was explosive and unpredictable. She told me the story about cutting Arthur's thumb and I was horrified. She definitely thought Arthur deserved it and was not at all remorseful.*

*At least she wasn't remorseful on the day she told me the story. It was just outrageous Connie behavior that seemed totally fine to her.  — Ann Henderling*

Connie's relationship with Dee Dee was pretty much over by then. She didn't even come around anymore, she was hardly ever at the shows because she was on heroin and she was a mess and they would fight a lot. I only remember her coming on any sort of tour one time. They took a picture of us somewhere, it was me and Connie and I think Dee Dee and Johnny were in the picture, too, it was in some paper. Usually the girls never got their pictures taken, it was just overlooked.

Connie was sort of tragic. She was always sad. She wasn't like the rest of us, she was older and tougher and she was a prostitute, not a dancer, but she wasn't a mean person. Everybody thought she was this horrible person because they'd heard these things, oh, she cut up Arthur and she cut up Dee Dee or whatever. She was very jealous of girls around her boyfriends, and she would get drunk and just go *nuts*, you know? She was a crazy drunk. She had an alcohol problem, definitely, but so what? So did everybody else! But she was actually very sweet. Connie never did anything bad to me. She was like a tragic figure, destined to die the way she did—alone.

Anyway, she moved in with me for a minute at the storefront and she wasn't around much, but Johnny didn't like her. One day he came over and said, "I want her stuff out of here, I don't want her staying here." And she listened to him, she just came and got her stuff and moved it away.

Later on, when Johnny and I lived on Tenth Street, I would run into her sometimes on Eighth Street. I'd be walking down the street shopping and there she was, a little high or whatever, and she would always ask me, "What's going on with Dee Dee?" I'd tell her what's going on, that he got married to the girl Vera who looked like her [*Dee Dee Ramone and Vera Boldis were married September 2nd, 1978.*]. And she would get sad and then she'd say, "Well, I'm gonna run in here and get a beer, give me money." So I'd buy her a beer and she'd drink it down real quick and want another one. And she'd get upset, she'd start crying, and then she'd disappear. She was prostituting on the street. She eventually got another boyfriend, Johnny Thunders' cousin. He was a real street hustler and a thief.

*Connie talked about Dee Dee Ramone all the time. They had broken up by then. She thought they might get back together. She talked a lot about Dee Dee and Germany, and Dee Dee being in the Luftwaffe. She thought it was very cool, the whole Germany thing. She bragged about Dee Dee a lot. Not about her relationship with Dee Dee, but just about his fabulousness in general. She loved him and they fought and finally he broke up with her. That's all she told me, really. I doubt she was easy to live with, but I do know she loved him. I don't think there is any secret that there were lots of drugs involved and lots of instability. Connie was violent sometimes, but Dee Dee was no mental health poster child, either.  — Ann Henderling*

*I didn't see Connie much after 1979/1980.
You would sometimes see her walking the
streets, hooking, but not so much at clubs. I
didn't frequent the late after-hours clubs, like
the Nursery, where she would hang out. ...
She was probably in a public hospital before
she died, and buried in Potters Field as an
indigent pauper ... Connie probably had
made at least a million during her life as a
stripper/hooker. So it is a very sad story. All
those people she supplied with drugs over the
years probably had no idea (or didn't care)
and no one who liked her (like the women on
the scene) knew where she was, or she had
scared them off by being crazy and violent.*

*— Eileen Polk*

Connie died in 1983. I don't know exactly how she died—probably
of a heroin overdose on the street with some trick or something, or in a
motel room. Taken to the morgue, unidentified, you know? I told Johnny
about Connie's death and that he should at least call Dee Dee and let him
know.

*Connie died of an overdose. I think it was
around 1983, from Tuinal, but that might not
be right. I remember it as pills, not heroin.*

*— Ann Henderling*

*Then I was in Toronto and John called me. He*
*said, "Did you hear Tommy died?"*
*And I said, "Tommy?"*
*And he said, "No, Connie." I had misheard*
*him. Connie had overdosed. It was as bad as*
*you can imagine.*
*I said, "Oh." That's all I said to show any*
*emotions about anything.*
                                            *— Dee Dee Ramone*

⌘

**Anya** (Ms Chow Mein) seen smooching
in cars with Jonathan Paley. Is this his
rendition of Chinese Rock?...
            —*New York Rocker*, "Pressed Lips"

*By early summer 1976, Anya and I had set up*
*home at 101 St. Marks Place and began to*
*decorate it in pink and black. This was a great*
*place. It's now the restaurant Mogador. I had*
*a loft bed in the corner and my darkroom*
*underneath it, and Anya had a huge four-*
*poster bed draped in pink fabric in the center*
*of the apartment. Richard Rockwood lived*

*with Anya and me for awhile, and it was much*
*better for me when he lived with us, because*
*Anya picked on him all the time instead of*
*me! Richard was so shy and quiet I thought*
*he was gay. I hardly remember much of him*
*except he was English, very quiet, and he*
*was an artist—he drew beautiful flowers that*
*he sold to wallpaper companies. After I left,*
*Terence Sellers moved in, and later Sylvia*
*Morales, who ended up marrying Lou Reed.*

— *Eileen Polk*

Anya and Eileen Polk became roommates that summer, they lived in a
storefront, too. Anya moved Richard Rockwood in with her for a little
while, and then this girl named Terry [*Terence Sellers*], who was a
dominatrix, also lived there. That's when Anya really started dressing
like a dominatrix and hanging out with Diego [*artist/writer Diego Cortez
(James Curtis)*] and then she managed The Contortions [*pioneering
New York noise/no wave band*] and then James Chance [*saxophonist,
originally a member of The Contortions*]. I don't know much about her
relationship with James other than I think she dominated him! She told
me I should read some book that was written by a dominatrix, I forget the
name of it. I had just read *The Story of O*, so I was already going in that
direction.

    Anya was great, you know? She was very influential. She was a
true dominatrix and really influenced me into becoming a dominatrix. I
was one of the only girls around at that time who was into that scene. I
thought it was crazy until I tried it!

Anya, along with artist Diego Cortez and Steve
Mass, co-founded the Mudd Club in October
1978, which quickly became the main venue for
the downtown post-punk music and arts scene,
especially the "noise"/No New York bands of
the late 1970s and early '80s. Less successfully,
she also managed the seminal New York noise
band The Contortions, a relationship that ended
acrimoniously in 1979 [6].

I didn't really get to know James until later; we became pretty close
after Anya died in 1981. I cried when she died. But Johnny didn't—he
didn't seem to feel bad at all, even though he knew Anya and had liked
her before. By then he didn't like any of my friends. The only girl that he
wanted me, that he *allowed* me to hang around with or be friends with,
was Linda.

**Cheetah** and **Geeter** have jungle fever.
This match was made in the streets!
—*New York Rocker*, "Pressed Lips"

Johnny didn't particularly care for Gyda, and she didn't like him
either. Ha ha ha! She really didn't like him. They just didn't get along.
She didn't like the way he treated me, and she didn't take shit from guys
too much [7].

But God, Gyda hated me, too, when she first met me! She wanted to beat me up because we both had gone out and bought the same pair of boots. Back then we were very particular about our clothes and we didn't want anybody else wearing what we were wearing. She walked into Max's one night and saw me wearing these knee-high cowboy boots, white leather with silver stars at the top all the way around. They were really cool at the time, and she was wearing them, too. She looked at me and she said, "When did you buy those boots?" And I said, "Well, today!" And she said: "*What time?*" Ha ha ha! She wanted to make sure she had bought them before I did! I looked at her like she was *nuts*, you know? But she was going around telling everybody what a bitch I was for having these boots!

Anyhow, what happened? We got together at some point and we just started talking. We started going out to the movies or to eat or something, I don't know. Somehow we became friends after that, I guess because we both had boyfriends that were musicians.

> Everyone has been commenting on those two pint sized honeys caught cooing everywhere. Who? **Kelvin Kiely** (Mumps) and **Little Linda**. Oh. Love is strange...
> —*New York Rocker*, "Pressed Lips"

Linda Daniele was around too, but I didn't like her. She belonged to this little clique in New York that hated the cool clique that I was in. Fat Janis with the red hair, Janis Cafasso, that bitch! And AbbiJane, and Linda, "Little Linda," and Anna Sui [8]. Anna SOOOEY! Yeah, those girls hated me and Anya and Gyda. Especially they all hated Anya because Anya was fucking around with this guy Justin Strauss [*singer for the band Milk 'n' Cookies*], who was Abbi's boyfriend at the time. So what. Anya would get drunk and rowdy and start taking on our enemies, the other girls in the mix—like Janis, who wrote "Pressed Lips," the gossip column in the *New York Rocker*, which we all secretly read and loved. You were no one if you weren't mentioned in that column each month! All she did was insult us and praise her buddies Abbi-Jane and Little fucking Linda. They hated us because the guys loved us for what we were, crazy-ass strippers who would do anything.

But those girls were stuck-up and obnoxious, we had our little clique and they had theirs and they were everywhere and we were everywhere and we hated each other. Janis always wrote a bunch of crap about us in that gossip column of hers. We'd wait for this thing to come out each month to see what the hell she was going to say. And we'd go on and on about what an asshole she was, and "What's she gonna say next month?" It was in the back and everybody read it, it was like the first thing you'd turn to. First thing we would turn to!

Guys liked Linda because she was bubbly and very chatty. But she dressed like a clown, OK? Fiorucci, that's what she wore in New York, before she became a beautician. Everything she wore was Fiorucci. Her nose was like three times as big as it is now and she had a moustache! There's one picture of me and Johnny and Joey in California. They were wearing their ripped-up jeans and all that, and I'm reading a book, I've got I think ripped stockings on and a pair of Fredericks boots—nothing goes, but it's all I had. And there's Linda standing there in her Fiorucci outfit. And it's like, "Who is that fuckin' clown over in the corner?" She doesn't even look like she belongs with us! She thought she was some sort of fashion model or something. She was just ridiculous [9].

⌘

Over that summer, '76, I was looking for an apartment that would be decent enough for Johnny to move into that I could afford. I ended up taking a place on Irving Plaza, across from where Gyda was living—another apartment I wasn't supposed to be in! Then I went to California with Johnny and when I came back, that place was gone.

That was the Ramones' first tour of California [*August 1976*], the first tour they did after they came back from England. It was also the first time I travelled with them, and my first time in the van—the dreaded van! Monte [*Melnick, Ramones road manager*] and John drove. I read. I remember I brought my little poodle along, Egbert. Johnny named him after the W.C. Fields character, Egbert Sousé, but he always called him Shithead. The poor dog didn't last long—he was hit by a car in San Francisco a few days into the tour and died. Johnny laid his leather jacket over him and cried, I will never forget that.

But other than that, it was a good time. I remember staying at the Parc Plaza, Danny Fields [*Ramones co-manager, with Linda Stein*] was there, Tomata du Plenty [*former Cockette, then singer for L.A. punk band The Screamers*], guys from The Tubes, all these characters. That was the last time I saw Johnny get high. He was drinking and smoking pot and his friend Moon was sniffing glue. He got really fucked up and he couldn't talk, he was stumbling over his words and I was like, "Ahh, you're fucked up! Ha ha ha!" That was the last time. He used to drink a lot when I first met him, and he was a heroin addict before I knew him, when he was a teenager, before he married Rosana. Back when he was still in the neighborhood and didn't know what to do with himself.

# 1977

**JOHNNY RAMONE** follows the yo-yo syndrome, one night out with his wife, the next with **ROXY**. The latter has declared that Johnny is her new roomie. HMM.

**DEE DEE RAMONE**'s new year started off bleak but he has said it's getting brighter. After having his ass quartered for marketing by his girlfriend **CONNIE** who doubles as a butcher, I'm hoping '77 is a little less brutal for him...
—*New York Rocker*, "Pressed Lips"

[What] I remember about the stabbing is that Dee Dee claimed he was 'in the act' with a girl and Connie walked in and stabbed him in the ass with a Heineken bottle. (As least it was good beer!) The rumor was that he was with Nancy Spungen. I don't know if that is true or not. Connie told everyone he was 'fucking a boy'—but that could have been just to humiliate him. Connie was great at that! [But] Dee Dee was a sex god and fucked everybody he could! — Eileen Polk

The Ramones were on tour in California and Colorado from mid-February to mid-March 1977 (including a week at the Whisky in LA with Blondie, Feb. 16–20), to promote *Ramones Leave Home*, the band's second album, which had been released January 10. Roxy and Johnny started living together after this tour.

The ass-stabbing incident happened sometime between late January and mid-February; Dee Dee was still walking with a cane when the Ramones left for California. The stabbing occurred on the third floor of the old Hotel Earle, 103 Waverly Place (currently the Washington Square Hotel). Coincidentally, Arthur Kane was also living in the hotel at the time, on the fifth floor, with his new girlfriend and soon-to-be wife, Barbara, who recalls that Dee Dee ran to their room after being stabbed [1]. It is doubtful that Dee Dee was with Nancy Spungen; she was almost certainly in London in January 1977, having gone to England in pursuit of Heartbreakers drummer Jerry Nolan. The Heartbreakers had arrived in England sometime before December 1, 1976 to join the Sex Pistols' "Anarchy in the UK" tour, replacing the Damned, who had been kicked off the tour for not being Marxist enough to suit Clash manager Bernie Rhodes. Spungen was definitely in London by late February 1977, when Sid Vicious joined the Sex Pistols; their relationship began at that time.

EARLY '77 IS WHEN JOHNNY actually moved in with me, to 85 East 10th St., #2Q. At the corner of 10th Street and 4th Avenue.

The rent was $305 a month. I don't know why I remember that, but I do! It was rent controlled. And it was a brand new building; nobody had ever lived there before. My mother sent the rent money every month, she helped us a lot. She loved John, except his violent temper. I could ask my family for anything and they'd send it to me. But Johnny pretty much took care of everything else besides the rent. He kept that place for a long, long time, I know that.

Up until then I had done a lot of drugs, mainly pills. Alcohol, meth, speed and downers. The first thing that happened when we moved in together was Johnny stopped everything. He gave up smoking pot, and I gave up all the pills I had lived on and pretty much sobered up into a quiet bookworm when I was around him and his band. That's the way he wanted me. No more flaunting myself and being the drunken flirt that I always was! We would have two beers at the end of the night and that was it. Sometimes I'd go on little binges and get completely fucked up, but then I'd stay sober again. Without my black beauties I would go right into drunk mode and black out, and I wasn't taking pills anymore, so I was mostly sober when I lived with him. I remember when I turned 21 we were walking down the street and he told me that I was no longer a child and that it was time for me to grow up. Him, telling *me* that! Well, we were both like children, I guess.

Then he started changing the way I dressed. He finally came out and told me he didn't like the way I dressed, even though it attracted him when he first met me. The corsets from Fredericks of Hollywood and the Springolators and black leather miniskirts, garter belts and stockings, lots of black and lots of make-up, magenta hair...I thought he liked that about me. But he told me he didn't like the way I dressed at all, he didn't like all that stuff. He wanted me to quit wearing corsets and stockings and all black. Then he started going with me to the stores to buy my clothes. He would pick out all my clothes, including my underwear. He liked me in white and pastels, so I gave away everything black or red, passed all my cool Ian's and SEX clothes down to Gyda. He even gave me an allowance at first: ten dollars a day. Ridiculous compared to what I had been making as an exotic dancer! But he didn't like me dancing. He told me he didn't want me to work, and I couldn't work and travel with him anyhow, so I stopped dancing. No work, no drugs, no cigarettes, and I had to stand where he could see me when he played! Then he didn't want me talking to anyone—no friends—until my "best friend" Linda came along.

We didn't even have a phone for a long time when we first moved in together. I had a phone in my name and he had run up a large phone bill calling from England or something and didn't want to pay it, and anyway it had been all my friends calling me, so he said we didn't need a phone! He used to make all his calls from the phone booth around the corner, at 4th Avenue and 11th St.

But at first I was happy, I was very happy. I didn't have to work anymore. Not that I really *had* to, but.

*Did any of you guys ever consider the military?*
**Johnny:** Yeah!! I wanted to be a soldier. So did Dee Dee. I wanted to go to military school, the battlefield, 'Nam...
**Tommy:** When I was a kid, I wanted to be in the air force.
**Dee Dee:** It's a good life.
**Joey:** I tried to join up, but they ah unh, said I'd have to kill geeks...unh, gooks. [much laughter] ...
—*New York Rocker*

Johnny showed me how to do things the way he liked them done. He showed me how to make a bed military style. He had gone to military school and had even thought about a career in the military, he liked that life and he liked doing things in an orderly way. He showed me how to do the laundry and fold his clothes, and I still fold clothes like that to this day. He set up a schedule for us at home, we had a time to do this, a time to do that. At a certain hour of the night—"OK, let's shut off the TV now, it's reading time!" And we would take out our books and we'd read! Yeah, reading time. Well, it was a good habit, reading. We read a lot of books, he wanted to have a library. Besides *The New York Post* and *T.V. Guide*, which he was nuts for, Johnny liked biographies and autobiographies, mostly of baseball and movie people, but he had lots of heroes he liked to read about.

Being regimented like that made things easy, and he liked things easy. I understand that, because I like things easy, too. He used to tell me that as soon as the band broke up he was going to get fat and grow a beard, he wasn't even going to bother to shave anymore. Because he had to shave twice a day, he always had 5 o'clock shadow. He would say, "I'll probably be bald by then, but I'll grow a beard and be able to eat what I want." He was just going to relax and let himself go. He was always talking about when he retires, he's gonna have his laundromat or his parking lot...whatever business would require him to do the least work!

I don't know much about the military school—it was somewhere on the east coast, maybe North Carolina? It was before he went to high school, by high school he was back in Forest Hills. I don't know how long he was there, but he talked about it like he'd been there all his life! [2] He would tell these horrible stories about what they made the kids do, and then he'd start laughing because he liked it, because he was sort of a sadist!

It was a boarding school, his parents sent him there I guess because he was such a bad kid. Johnny was a troublemaker and he had been in trouble with the law a few times, but military school didn't cure him of anything. After high school he got really bad. His college try in Fort Lauderdale came to nothing, he arrived with his guitar and his hairdo and they laughed him outta there. So he came right back to New York and turned into a juvenile delinquent. He liked to go out and do things to people, prank stuff. Stupid little jokes, mostly, but sometimes vicious things, too, like trapping old ladies in elevators or exposing himself to little girls. He lived in a Jewish neighborhood and he'd walk around and paint swastikas on stuff. He didn't know what to do with himself, so he started doing a lot of drugs, hard drugs—heroin. This was like the bad, low part of his life [3]. His girlfriend at the time was Arlene, who was Mitch's [*Mickey Leigh's*] girlfriend and wife later. She was from Forest Hills, too [4].

So then his parents took him to psychiatrists and they put him on Thorazine for a long time. He told me that the Thorazine was so strong he couldn't do anything, he didn't feel like doing anything. He became a zombified couch potato, he didn't want to work, he was just sitting and watching television and eating and he put on weight and he became like a walking dead. Finally I guess the psychiatrist told his parents that he was a hopeless case and that he couldn't do anything for Johnny. And Johnny said that when he heard what the doctor had told his parents, he wanted to totally do the opposite and show them that this guy was an idiot and didn't know anything. He said that's when he decided he was going to straighten up his life, get a job, get married and own a Rolls-Royce. Goals, you know.

*I had my leather jacket since '67. I was a real punk. I was a bad person, then all of a sudden one day I woke up. I didn't like who*

*I was. I gave up drinking and drugs. After
two years, I just woke up. [Before that,] I'd
see a bottle in the street and put it through
someone's window. Just petty things that
were wrong. I didn't like who I was. I went to
see a psychiatrist but after a while he said,
"I can't help you."... I thought, "What are you
going to do with your life? I don't know what
the hell I want to do." I decided the next day I
was going to find a part-time job. Held that for
six months and then went to my father and
said I was ready for a full-time job. He was in
construction. Then Affirmative Action came
around and they needed to fill a quota really
quick on a job that was all white and I lost my
job. Then I went out and bought a guitar.*
                                        *— Johnny Ramone*

Our life together was pretty normal. We went to a lot of baseball
games, went to a lot of movies, went shopping, collected movie posters
and memorabilia, records, clothes… He liked to collect things. I gave
him these sets of baseball cards that my brothers had saved when
they were kids. They were all in perfect condition, they'd never been
touched—they were in the plastic or whatever they came in. After he got
those, he just went on this binge of collecting stuff! It started with the
baseball cards, then he started collecting baseballs, then they had to be
autographed by baseball players, then it was baseball teams, then it was
presidents of the United States...! Then it was pictures of movie stars,
and old horror and sci-fi movie posters. By the time he died, I understand

he had one of the best collections of movie posters ever [5].

He would get those Leonard Maltin books that came out every year, with all the reviews of the movies, and every year when he bought the new one we would have to sit down and he would have me go through the book with him—Ha ha ha, this is crazy, but we'd go through each page and he would have me mark down every movie he'd seen, because his goal was to see as many movies as he could in his lifetime. He wanted to see every movie. He had a vast knowledge of movies and movie actors and trivia. Later, when it became known that he was a huge horror fan, young directors would send him their films, we had a vast collection of those. He also bought a lot of old 8mm films of Buster Keaton, Laurel & Hardy, The Three Stooges and Harold Lloyd, along with a projector, which at the time was the only way to watch these films. We eventually got a videotape machine and when he would go away for a day or a weekend, he would write out a detailed schedule of movies he wanted me to tape for our collection, usually old Marx Brothers or W.C. Fields comedies. This would also guarantee that I would be at home in the apartment while he was gone, doing this chore for him—and I had better do it right.

Yeah, movies were a big part of our life, movies and baseball. We went to a lot of Yankees games. Or any sport, he was really into sports. In 1986, when I was living in Chicago, he came out for my birthday and took me to a wrestling match. That's the kind of stuff we did.

There were a lot of things Johnny wanted to do before he died. He wanted to cram as much into life as he could. He thought he was going to live to be a hundred, we both thought he was going to live a long time. And he *should* have lived a long time—it's so ridiculous that he would die so young, of such a treatable cancer! Why wasn't he taken to see a doctor? Well, I know why: he hated doctors. He never went to a doctor, ever. It's so crazy. He just *would not go*. And he had health insurance— it wasn't that! I mean, I kept asking him to get *me* health insurance, because when I'd get sick, I would always run to the doctor. I don't like being sick. That's why I juiced every day and used herbs, natural remedies, homeopathics. I was a fanatic about nutrition back then, I knew a lot about it. I was a drug addict, but I knew a lot about health! Johnny called it all my "crazy stuff" and thought I was a little nuts. But I would tell him what vitamins to take, and he would do that—he would take vitamins and minerals, stuff you could get in the health food store. He would go to the health food store, but he wouldn't go to a doctor. So at least I got him started on taking vitamins and eating certain foods to keep him healthy for a long time, like eating sardines every day, which was supposed to keep you young. And wheat grass juice. We would stop by the juice bar at our neighborhood health food store every day.

His big concern was his hair—he was always worried about his hair. If he went into a swimming pool, he would swim with his head above the water so he didn't get his hair wet. He wanted to make sure he never lost his hair, he never wanted to go bald. He had already stopped smoking pot almost altogether and cut back on drinking to two beers a night, then he started taking a tremendous amount of B vitamins every day. At some point I remember Linda saying, "Oh, I wanna learn about vitamins too," so he went out and bought her one of the books that I had given him. Even though all she ever did was look at pictures in fashion magazines!

But he was very careful about what he ate, and he didn't smoke, he didn't drink, he didn't take drugs, and he tried to keep his body in good shape. He tried to exercise and do what's right. He wanted to live a long time. He really did.

*[D]o you believe in jogging?*
**EEEaaahhh—I always *want* to, but I'm too lazy.**
**Once in a while I get up and go run round**

**my block and want to, but then I always say
"That's enough". People start to look and say,
"Hey, Johnny!" y'know? "What're ya doin'?"
Everybody recognizes ya every time ya go
outta the house, everybody on every block so,
ah, I feel silly. "Hey, what're ya doin'—jogging?
Who're ya runnin' from, hmmmm?" You
know?   — Johnny Ramone**

We also used to go out to eat a lot because I didn't cook. He bought
me a ton of cookbooks when we first got together because he wanted me
to learn how to cook for him. Like make breakfast. Well, I tried and it
didn't work out, ha ha ha! I think I put butter in the pan to make bacon
or something, I don't know, it just didn't turn out. That was it for the
cooking lessons—after that, he went across the street every morning
before I woke up to eat at this greasy spoon, and he was very happy and I
was happy, too. I never learned how to cook and never wanted to.

There were jokes or whatever about the Ramones only eating
hamburgers but Johnny never ate hamburgers. He liked Mexican food,
and then I taught him about other foods, like Japanese and Indian. He
had never tried Indian before but I love it, and after a while he ended up
liking it, too [6].

The other thing we did a lot together was fight. We were known for
that—they called us the "Battling Ramones" because we'd be outside
CBGB, going at it. We had major fights, fistfights. Black eyes and
bruises. One time we had a big fight at home and he threw me into the
shower with my clothes on. The cops came over to our house but they
just laughed. Everybody saw us fighting. I guess they were afraid to even
say anything because that's the way he was, he really enjoyed punching

and fighting, especially in public. But then he would cry afterwards if I had a bruise, and tell me it wouldn't happen again.

I was pretty bad, too. I started fights with him a lot. I liked to provoke him. To me it was kind of sexual, it fit into the whole B&D thing and it was exciting. We were living like master and slave if you ask me—that's sort of what I was looking for at the time. I don't know what his feelings were, but for me violence and sex went together, and I looked for men who would push me around and leave marks. We didn't get into real S&M, although I remember Johnny whipping me with the phone cord once—after we *got* a phone—but I loved being an outlet for his anger and aggression. I'd walk around with the bruises and black eyes and be proud of them, thinking it meant true love.

And it did. Johnny fell hard for me because I was what he wanted, too: a hard-core punk rebel who was a sexual masochist to his sadistic tendencies and tough exterior. We looked good together. And I loved his possessiveness and jealousy. He ruled my life with an iron fist, no two ways about it. He owned me. That's why I gave all my clothes away and allowed him to choose what he wanted me to wear, down to my little white panties. He was a bit of a pedophile, one of his favorite fantasies was very young girls with large breasts, so he used to dress me up like a little girl, in pastel or white soft, short dresses or a very short skirt and a blouse, and white cotton panties. He got off on the cotton underwear. He'd put ribbons in my hair, and I'd wear lace-trimmed ankle socks and white strappy high-heeled shoes. He would go shopping with me, I could not go alone, and he would touch all the fabric of the panties and little dresses and choose the ones he'd like for me to wear. I was his slave, he was my master. That's how I learned—that was my training to become the professional dominatrix that I am now.

Everyone saw a tremendous change in me. For good or bad, who knows? I'd probably be dead myself if not for him.

*She loved it, y'know. She was into it. It was part of the allure. It was the dynamics of their relationship, that's essentially what it became: master and slave.  — Gyda Gash*

We were really so much alike it was sort of sickening. We liked and disliked the same things, we were like the same person in a lot of ways. We would say the same things all the time, finish each others' sentences, and the longer we were together, the more alike we became.

⌘

**Tommy:**  Johnny didn't tell his parents he was in the Ramones until the [first] record was in the stores.
**NYR:**  Why is that?
**Johnny:**  Cause I knew they didn't want me to play and I didn't want to bother them.  *—New York Rocker*

The first time I saw his parents was when they came to the Palladium to see him play [*October 1977, opening for Iggy Pop; also the first time Johnny's parents saw the band*] [7]. I remember his mother had curlers in her hair, pink rollers, which I thought was a little strange. I walked into the dressing room and his dad turned around and looked at me and his eyes lit up and he was like, "Oh hey, Johnny, who's this girl?" John practically pushed the two of them out of the room because he was still married and didn't want them to see me, although his dad was looking right at me and it was pretty obvious he was with me!

That was the only time I ever saw his dad, and Johnny quickly *whooshed* me into another room. He didn't want them to know about me. His father died before I ever got to meet him because Johnny kept trying to keep me a secret. [*Johnny's father Frank Cummings died May 5, 1979*]. He always had to have a secret life. Before me, he had a secret life with Arlene on the side, while he was married to Rosana. It was a pattern that he had to do, or wanted to do. It gave him a thrill or something, it was how he got his kicks. How many women could he string along and make love him, then start sneaking around with another one. Of course, his mother knew he lived with some girl. His mother's name was Stella Krasig—she was Ukrainian or Polish. [*Johnny's mother, Estelle "Stella" Krasig Cummings, passed away in Florida in June 2012.*]

Johnny was born in Westbury, Long Island, but his parents moved to Forest Hills when he was young. He was an only child. Frank Cummings had owned a bar when Johnny was little, and Johnny used to wait up for him to come home at 2 or 4 in the morning, then he would carry Johnny around the block on his shoulders and let him drink a can of beer. Johnny told me he went to a Yankees game with his father once when he was a kid and he drank three cans of beer and passed out. His dad had three brothers that all looked exactly like him—very Irish, fat, with that Johnny nose. His father ended up being a construction worker so I don't know what happened to the bar. He was probably an alcoholic, but he never drank around Johnny's mother, and then he stopped cold turkey when they moved to Florida, which is probably what caused his sudden heart attack. Johnny's parents moved down to Kissimmee, Florida, as soon as his father retired, and he quit drinking because he only drank at work and he didn't go to work anymore. A couple of months later he had a heart attack and died. Johnny was devastated, he really adored his father. It was one of the only times I ever saw him cry over someone's death—that, and when John Wayne died and when Elvis died. I remember Stella gave Johnny a ring that had belonged to his father. He's wearing it in the "Psychotherapy" video, I think that's the only time he ever wore any jewelry.

> *[Johnny's] parents wanted him very much not to be involved with music. They wanted him to be a baseball player. They thought music was effeminate or wasn't at all American. His sense of American patriotism and right-wing thinking comes from his parents, from identifying with his father. When his father died in 1979, it was a big change for him.*
> — *Tommy Ramone*

As far as his mother, Johnny couldn't be around her for very long. I remember the first time I met her. She had flown back up to New York and she wanted to meet him for lunch or something and he brought me along, he was finally going to introduce me to her. I'd only been living with him for, what, I don't know how many years!

So we all went out to eat. We were sitting at a table outdoors somewhere and talking, and then she started crying. This was right after her husband died and she was depressed. Whenever his name was brought up or anything, she would start crying. Johnny couldn't deal with it, so he got up and walked away and left me sitting with her. I felt bad for her. I knew what she was going through, because my mother went through the same thing. Then she turned to me and said, "How long have you been living with him?" And I said, "Well, it's been years, you know!" Ha ha ha! I think it was two or three years by then. She goes, "Well, I knew that."

She knew—Johnny thought she didn't. He was pretty naive about things like that. Then she started telling me how much she couldn't stand Rosana. I didn't like to talk bad about anyone, but she was going on about how she couldn't stand that whole family, and "Oh, that Jew bitch," and all this shit.

I thought we got along fine. I was always respectful to her. Johnny couldn't deal with her too much. She talked a lot and she would kind of nag him a little bit, but not really; she was just being a mother and trying to take care of him. She fussed over him, and why not? She was very proud of him. She used to buy him all his clothes, she would send him packages of underwear, socks, sneakers—and he got all those T-shirts for free, so he never had to buy any clothes ever! She just couldn't do enough for him.

*My mom always treated me like a star. I was her only kid. My father would go on these [rants] about how he never missed a day's work. I broke my big toe the day before I had to go pitch a Little League game and he's going, "What are you—a baby?["] ... And even though my toe was broken, I had to go pitch the game anyway. It was terrible. It would always be like that. I'm glad he raised me*

*that way, but it would always be, "What are*
*you—sick? You're not sick. What did I raise—a*
*baby? I never missed a day's work in my life."*
                                    *— Johnny Ramone*

Johnny's father had been a construction worker, he was in the union, and that's how Johnny got into construction work for a while—his father got him that job. Johnny and his father would go to work in the morning and as soon as they got there, his father would start drinking and continue drinking all day. Johnny said he never saw his father do any work. Then he'd go home at night and he wouldn't touch any alcohol in the house. First thing in the morning they would go out, and he would start drinking again. I guess he didn't want to drink in front of his wife.

One of Johnny's construction jobs was at 1633
Broadway at 50th Street, where his friend Douglas
Colvin, soon to be known as Dee Dee Ramone,
also worked, as a mail clerk at Employers
Insurance of Wausau. They often met for lunch.

*Johnny Ramone and I really had no intention*
*of ever playing in groups ... We were happy*
*just taking the subway to work every day,*
*going to Chock Full O' Nuts [old time New*

*York chain diner] and the Metropole for lunch*
*to watch the go-go dancers and drink a beer.*
*... John liked Geri Miller, the go-go dancer*
*Andy Warhol star. She was dancing at the*
*Metropole and we'd go spy on her.*
                                    *— Dee Dee Ramone*

The whole time Johnny was working with his dad he never spent
any money. He lived with his parents, he took the subway to work, he
would go with his little lunch bag to the construction site—he brought
lunch with him, he never bought anything. He saved all his money to
buy this damn Rolls-Royce he wanted, so he could impress girls and get
himself into Max's Kansas City. Johnny had a vendetta against Max's
because he had tried to go there once with his wife and they wouldn't let
him in. This is a true story and it really had an effect on him, I guess. He
wasn't cool enough or whatever, they overlooked him in line, and he got
so mad that he said he was going to start a band and someday the doors
would be open for him. He was going to become somebody so that he
would never have to stand in line and be embarrassed like that again.

Well, he didn't buy a Rolls-Royce, he bought a Jaguar. But he didn't
have a driver's license, nor did he know how to drive, so he had Dee Dee
go and take the license test for him. Back then there were no pictures on
driver's licenses, so Dee Dee took the test for him, and then went with
him to get the car and drove the car home from the lot for Johnny.

But the car didn't go over too well—Jaguars are sort of
temperamental. He thought he was gonna get this impressive car and
he was gonna start this band, and he was gonna be cool and be let into
Max's Kansas City. Except the car never worked! It kept breaking down.
He didn't know anything about cars to begin with, so why he would get

a car that would be so hard to fix, I don't know. It sounded like it broke down every time he took it out. Finally he just dumped the Jaguar and got a Chevy Vega—that's what he owned when we started seeing each other. He just wanted to get the cheapest car he could, after that lemon! Same with his guitar, he bought a really cheap guitar.

Johnny Ramone's first guitar was a blue Mosrite, purchased at Manny's Music on 48th Street in midtown Manhattan for $54.55 ($50 + 4.55 tax) on January 23, 1974. This guitar was stolen in 1977 while the band was in Chicago. According to Ramones legend, Dee Dee went with Johnny and bought his first bass, a Danelectro, that same day. The Ramones first-ever performance (as a trio, with Joey Ramone on drums and Dee Dee singing) was two months later, on March 30 at Performance Studio.

*I wanted a guitar that no one else was using, I wanted to be identified with a guitar. They made a mistake [at Manny's] on the price of the guitar. They had quoted me seventy dollars or something. I asked them about ten others and when we got back to the Mosrite, I asked them again how much it was and they said it was fifty dollars, so I took it thinking I was getting one over on them. ... It was a good guitar for me. Lightweight, very thin neck, easy to barre chord. It just had a sound of its own. I was happy with it. Later on I met Mr. [Semi] Moseley [creator of the Mosrite] and he was very nice to me.* — Johnny Ramone

*We used to check out the guitars on 48th Street together. Johnny Ramone never broke a guitar. He couldn't be bothered. He found one he liked and always played the same one. ... Still, it's sort of strange to play sick music on a Mosrite, which is really supposed to be a surf guitar. Somehow they're all right to use with fuzz tones and stuff. They also go very well with bowl haircuts.* — Dee Dee Ramone

I don't know what he was thinking about the guitar. He bought it because somebody else played that guitar, that's what he told me—some guitar player he liked. [*Besides surf heroes The Ventures, who made it famous, Fred "Sonic" Smith of the MC5 also played a Mosrite.*] He went to Manny's and I think it was fifty dollars, but it looked cool. And he practiced his little Wayne Kramer spins and moves all the time. Didn't matter whether he could play it or not, he just had to look cool! He never tried to progress with his music or anything, he didn't practice—he hated that. When he was in the house, he never picked it up or anything.

*I have never improved since I started playing
and I don't want to do. I always thought that
he who changes, changes for the worst;
only the Beatles changed with success from
album to album.* — Johnny Ramone

He kept his guitars right under the bed, a couple of them. Once in a while he would take it out and he would just go: *dih-daaaaah*—"Hey listen to this:" *daaaaahh—Eeeeeeee*—y'know? And that would be it! But he never really practiced. You're around musicians, like when I lived with Marc, he always had drumsticks in his hand and he would beat on anything close to him, you know? Most musicians do that sort of shit. But not Johnny. They would maybe rehearse for a couple of hours a day or whatever and that was it. That was enough.

We listened to a lot of music at home, he had a big record collection. Of course, he never opened them—just kept them sealed on a locked bookshelf. He listened to *my* punk records! We liked the Cramps, Plasmatics, the Dickies. He also liked Leslie West [*aka Leslie Weinstein, guitarist of Mountain, who was also from Forest Hills*] and Wayne Kramer [*MC5*], the Beatles, old stuff. But he hated the Clash and Sex Pistols because he felt they were competition. He broke my Clash records! I listened to music all the time, but my records were all beat up and scratched up and I had some cheap stereo system. His were in perfect condition, like they'd never been played. And he never did play them!

Then we started collecting records. As we were touring around the country we'd go to the local record shops and buy all these records for like fifty cents apiece, sealed and everything, and we'd have boxes and boxes when we got home. He had this cabinet made with locks on it and he would put all his records in there and lock 'em up so I couldn't touch them. He kept everything separated. He had his books in one place, I had my books in another place, because my books were underlined and written in—you could tell that I *read* all my books! But everything of his had to be in perfect condition, so he would lock all his stuff up. I remember I broke into his cabinet once. He came home and some of his records were, like, underneath the furniture, ha ha ha! He just went nuts!

In some ways I guess he liked that I was a little crazy. I think a lot of men like that, to balance things off. But I can be very controlled and very organized, too, in my own way. He valued my opinion and always asked my opinion in private. At one point I inherited a lot of money from my father and Johnny was worried I wouldn't need him anymore, he didn't like the fact that I had all that money. I invested in Fidelity mutual funds, just like he did. Then I started advising him on which ones to buy, because I paid $100 a year for a newsletter from some genius and he was always right. That's the kind of thing Johnny would never do, but he'd let me do it, or expect me to research it for us. He called it all my "crazy things," like herbal remedies, Bach flower essences, massage, acupuncture, yoga, high colonics, all the health-oriented shit I was interested in. He would make fun of me, but he would listen to me, too. He always told me, "You're the smartest person I know." He wouldn't say that in front of other people—if he was talking to someone and I tried to say something, he'd just go, "Oh shut up, asshole." But that was on the outside. At home, we talked about everything.

It shocked me and it hurt me when he would talk to me like that, but if I complained about it, we'd usually get into a fight. Or he would say he needed to talk to the fans and I should understand that, because these are the people who bought his records. But it wasn't just the fans, it was everybody—he would never introduce me to anyone. Really, he felt that nobody should even know who I am, because I'm *nobody*. I was just his girlfriend. So I would just stand there and say nothing, like an idiot. It was like the girlfriends didn't exist.

> *Johnny...had a very low opinion of women—all*
> *women. He considered them inferior and*
> *insignificant and thought they should be seen*
> *but not heard. Never in all those years did he*
> *acknowledge the opinions of any of the wives*
> *or girlfriends, until Linda came along.*
> — *Vera Ramone*

And it wasn't just Johnny. Dee Dee seemed like an asshole, too, always beating up Vera, making her get down in the dirt "where she belonged," and pulling knives on her. Joey was sort of quiet and Linda was always in everybody's face. She took charge of everything in Joey's life because he was so fuckin' chaotic and couldn't handle anything. I mean, she used to stand there and hold his pants open so he could he step into them, like a little child. It was embarrassing. And she always had her big mouth going. Whereas I knew to keep my mouth shut till I was asked a question.

But at home, or when we were alone, Johnny was like a different person. No matter what anybody says or what they thought, he valued my opinions and listened to me when we were alone. Maybe I didn't talk to anybody else or didn't talk at all when we were around other people, but he and I talked together. He talked *everything* over with me. Everything! As I say, he always told me I was the smartest person he knew. But then, look who he was hanging around with!

In private, Johnny was sweet, light-hearted and kind to me. He brought me flowers all the time. We always bought a lot of gifts for each other on holidays and birthdays. And he used to tell me all his business. He made sure that I knew how much money he had and where it was. When they were going out on tour, he'd write down the numbers of the bank account and everything, in case the plane went down. He even set up a trust fund for me years ago—I don't know what happened to it, but I know that at one point, he had put away $65,000 for me. He wanted to make sure I was taken care of. But as soon as I went to prison I never heard from him again, which was strange.

⌘

**Johnny:** I was out of work collecting unemployment. I always wanted to be a rock star, but I knew there was something wrong about it. I shouldn't want to be a rock star because it's sick, so I tried to get it out of my head.
**Tommy:** I used to call John once a month and say, "Hey, John, you want to be a rock star?" He'd say "Don't bother me."
**Johnny:** I don't know. I just didn't want to do it. I just knew there was something wrong—evil about it.
**NYR:** Has it proven to be evil?
**Johnny:** It's eviler than I ever thought it was.
**Tommy:** It's as evil as anybody ever thought. [Group laughter]
                          —*New York Rocker*

I guess he thought it was bad to want to be in a rock band because it's not normal. You don't live a normal life. But for him being in a rock band, we lived a pretty normal, boring life—he tried to keep it as normal as possible. Even though he was around a lot of freaky people, he didn't want to be like that himself. He was uncomfortable with and disliked anything that was too "different."

Like for example, Johnny really *was* a racist—that was no joke. He did not like blacks. He did not understand them and possibly was afraid of them. He was never around any to begin with! Maybe that's why. When Monte was driving the van, he would always say, "Ten points if you hit the nigger." But he was racist against everybody else, too—the chinks, the heebs, the spics! His dad was very racist, and all his uncles who all looked exactly alike. They looked like a meeting of the Teamsters when they got together. So Johnny would mimic the stuff that his dad and his uncles would say. And even though he made a big deal of being a Ronald Reagan supporter, he never registered to vote because he didn't want to be called for jury duty! Which kept happening anyway, but he always got out of it. He made *me* register, so that I could vote for Ronald Reagan for him! I remember I registered in Illinois, since my driver's license was from there, and I voted, I think for the only time in my life, by absentee ballot, for Reagan—for Johnny.

Johnny was a capitalist, that's why he went with being a Republican, and he liked Reagan because he was an old-time actor. I guess he was always star-struck about actors. At one time we had a huge collection of signed 8 x 10 photos of older movie stars, from Lillian Gish to Brigitte Bardot. He went to a lot of trouble writing to them all and getting them to autograph these photos.

He would collect things, but he didn't want much to do with people. It seems like he changed a little afterwards, but when I was with him, we just kept to ourselves and didn't hang out with any other rock stars or movie stars or anything like that. Johnny and I led very boring lives!

We didn't go to parties or meet people, it wasn't like that for us. He didn't *want* to meet anybody. Some of it had to do with his resenting the way the music business treated the Ramones. He *hated* music awards shows—we both did—of course, we still watched them! We used to watch the Grammys and he'd get so mad at all the mainstream shit getting awards. Like the year they gave Best Hard Rock/Metal Performance to Jethro Tull. That was hilarious!

He was also very upset that the Ramones were never asked to be on *Saturday Night Live*, especially being from New York and all. They never invited them on, even though Dan Aykroyd and John Belushi would come to their shows as the Blues Brothers and dance on the side. Johnny was so upset that they bypassed them for Blondie, the B-52s, and everybody else that he wouldn't let me watch the show! I guess it didn't hurt their ratings much. We watched SCTV instead, which he loved. He also loved MadTV, later on. He was very big on comedy.

But as far as socializing, he couldn't stand to hang around with other musicians. He thought they were dumb, or snobbish. Underneath it all, he really thought his own talent didn't go a long way. I remember, it might have been Cheetah Chrome or some other guitar player coming over and they would immediately want to pick up the guitar he stored under the bed—one of his Mosrites, I think the white one. I know Johnny Angel [*from Boston band The Thrills*] played it every chance he got. But Johnny Ramone would never have done something like that, because he wasn't real confident about his own playing at the time.

Anyway, even though it wasn't the glamorous life, I was happy and it was a good time, definitely. I enjoyed being alone with him. The best times were probably traveling to Europe with them, going overseas—that was fun. Going through customs could be a little tricky, but Joey was usually the target—they always made him strip because they figured he was for sure on drugs and most likely trying to smuggle something in or out. Poor Joey! He had a hard enough time getting in and out of his clothes. And one time in Sweden, Joey ended up paying $300 for breakfast at the hotel because he didn't understand the convesion of the money. But they treated us well in other countries, and John and I would spend time together, shopping for our collections.

In the U.S., we were always sightseeing. We went to H.P. Lovecraft's house in Rhode Island, the Amityville Horror house, *The Exorcist* house in Georgetown. He made sure we visited Elvis's mansion when we were down South, we took lots of pictures there. We would stop at any attraction along the road—two-headed snakes, lost mines, whatever, we were game! We especially loved carnivals and zoos, we loved animals and Johnny was always buying me stuffed toys and dolls. We bought all sorts of knick-knacks and crap at Stuckey's and Indian reservations, and collected science fiction masks like Yoda and Darth Vader, and of course we would come home with boxes and boxes of books and records, his favorite buys.

But they toured non-stop. It seemed like we were never home much anymore. Some of those shows, especially in the beginning, it was like they booked them *anywhere!* Take a little tiny aircraft up to the middle of the woods and play for some lumberjacks! Out of the way little bars, like, where did they *find* these places? Literally, I remember taking this tiny plane to some logging city in Washington State. First the journey itself was hair-raising, then there was the looks of the native inhabitants of the backwoods bar! The guys did their set and then we planned to scram outta there. Well, these big boys weren't having that—they wanted encore after encore as they continued their drinking!

Of course, it made sense to play every little club and bar they could, because the punk thing wasn't mainstream in any way. There was no punk scene except in New York—well, actually, there *was*, but it was really small, and the fact that the Ramones made the effort to go to their fans meant everything to them. That's part of the reason why the band has lasted so long. They really *did* play every little town, and people loved them for it and came out to see them wherever they played. They had their group of people that would come to every show, so every show was sold out. They had very loyal fans from the beginning.

> How do you guys feel about being
> up here? [*Utica NY*]
> DEE DEE:  Eh.
> TOMMY:  Um.
> JOHNNY:  Miserable!
> JOEY:  Heh! Heh!
> > —*illiterature*

The routine was always the same, they would warm up for an hour before the show, run the whole set. Tuning up, stretching, Joey doing his vocal things and steam, drinking tea. Interviews and hangers-on. Going onstage, Joey was always bumping into the other guys. He was so blind and wore those dark glasses, and besides not being able to see he would stop and take a step back because of his OCD and step on someone. They looked like the Three Stooges, running into each other! During the show it was really funny to watch when Dee Dee would lose his place in a song or start playing a different song than what they were supposed to be playing. John would get so angry—if looks could kill! He would stand there glaring away at him and playing fast and furious, and then after the set sometimes he would run up on Dee Dee and punch him. Dee Dee wouldn't even defend himself, he just took it from John. He knew he was wrong. Everyone else would just scatter.

And it was true that Johnny would pee into beer bottles and then set them down backstage, hoping someone would pick one up and drink it. I remember Dee Dee did, one night. John thought it was hilarious!

Traveling with them was fucked up. It really was like traveling with a bunch of retarded children. Poor Monte took so much abuse! He was pretty good-natured for all the ribbing he took: "Lamby eyes," "Monte Maps," that's what they called him. Marc used to give it to him the worst, but it wasn't mean-spirited. Tommy was the most sane, he and his girlfriend Claudia [*Tienan*], who became his wife. They were together forever.

I knew Claudia before she was with Tommy. She changed for him, too. She was like a groupie girl when I met her, always out, dressed really cool, really wild, all these nice clothes. She was real young, pretty, and then when she started going out with Tommy, all she wore was jeans and a leather jacket, ha ha ha! Which I refused to do. She looked real plain. But I liked Claudia, she was very quiet.

Anyway, the two of them couldn't stand riding in the van and couldn't wait till we stopped so they could chain-smoke. Johnny was like the Gestapo and would only stop when we needed gas, or after so many miles or hours. I don't remember how long but it was long and painful and if the guys wanted to pee between stops they had to pee in a bottle. The girls were shit out of luck. Once in a while we'd pull off to the side of the road, but that was only when John needed to pee. I used to have pictures of him peeing against the van. Tommy and Claudia would just be hangin' on till the next town we would stop. They were nervous wrecks and the road life was *not* for them, especially when arguments would break out in that little van. Like the time Dee Dee got into a fight with Vera because she wouldn't buy him the *Soldier of Fortune* magazine or whatever the fuck it was he wanted. He pushed her down on the floor of the van—mind you, there wasn't much floor space in there—and he was yelling, "Get down in the dirt where you belong, bitch!" We were tittering, John and I, and I think Monte said, "Isn't anyone going to help that poor woman?" It was pretty funny.

When Vera wasn't around and Dee Dee was alone, he'd get high and talk to other women. I don't know where Dee Dee met her, but it was almost like he was looking for someone to "channel" Connie. Vera did look a bit like Connie, but the resemblance ended there; she was a typical middle-class Long Island girl who drove a Trans Am and loved to sport her diamond ring from Dee Dee. He thought, for some crazy reason, that she would keep him sober plus take care of him. And she did—or tried to, as best anybody could. She did it pretty well for a while. Really, I felt sorry for Vera; she did *not* know what she was getting herself into.

*There was one incident that occurred in Dallas, Texas, after we left a 7-11 store where we had stopped for snacks. As we got back in the van, for no reason at all, Dee Dee started beating me, pulling chunks of hair from my head, punching me in the face until he had me on the floor of the van, and stomping on my head with his steel-tipped punk boots. What did I do? Was it my fault that they were out of his brand of cigarettes? Everyone just watched, and no one came to my rescue.*

*Finally Monte said, "Someone stop him before he kills her," to which Johnny responded, "Stay out of it! This is a domestic dispute." ...*

*The next morning ... [m]y eyes and face were so swollen I couldn't see. It hurt to even put sunglasses on my face before I took a*

*cab to the airport and got on a flight back
to New York. Even as I sat on the plane the
stewardesses looked at me and asked if they
could get me some medical help. ... My entire
body was bruised like I had been in a tragic
car crash.  — Vera Ramone*

Johnny wanted me to be with him all the time, so he made sure that the record company had plane tickets and everything for me and that I was traveling with him. And because I was there, all the other guys were able to bring their girlfriends, too. He couldn't say no to them and have me going! So they all brought somebody with. Dee Dee and Vera, and Tommy and Claudia. Marc and Marion. And Joey didn't have anybody. He was alone. Until he met Linda.

Joey and Linda Daniele got together when the Ramones were in California in February '77. We were staying at the Tropicana and Joey ran into Linda at Duke's Coffee Shop [*Duke's was a famous Los Angeles rock 'n' roll hangout, located on Santa Monica Boulevard next to the Tropicana Motel*]. She had moved out here to L.A. with AbbiJane's ex-boyfriend, Justin Strauss, from the band Milk'n'Cookies. Then she started hanging around Joey. Next thing you know, she's left Justin for Joey. Before this, Joey had a beautiful girl named Cindy—she was really pretty. Cindy lived in New York for a little while but she became a heroin addict and then she disappeared. Johnny hated her for some reason, *hated* her. God, I remember Johnny was going to hit her one night! She was always cocky and didn't put up with any bullshit. She's dead now; she OD'd.

I don't know how Linda knew Joey, but Joey knew everybody and she was around. And I guess he was the one who was without someone, so she just moved right in on him. Of course she was very outgoing and bubbly and all that.

I couldn't stand her—well, I'd never really talked to her. She was that other girl who hung out with Janis and AbbiJane, and they didn't like me and Anya and Gyda, so I didn't talk to her when I saw her. But out of that trio of Janis and Abbi and Linda, it seemed like she was just sort of hanging around with them. Everybody knew Janis and Abbi, Janis was a writer and she had been Johnny Thunders' girlfriend for a while, and Abbi was a designer, and Linda didn't do anything, she just came out of the blue and started tagging along with them. Then when Abbi broke up with Justin, Linda jumped in there and became his girlfriend. So it seems like she has that history of trying to jump in on her friends' boyfriends.

> *Joey was a very lonely guy. He didn't get too many girls, very shy. And she worked her way in there, y'know? There was a lot of fuckin' conversations at the bar. That was a major accomplishment. That's how she got in. Then she went for the next vulnerable entity, and that was Roxy. And she worked her way into that, and that's how she landed the big bonus prize. The bronze statue. — Gyda Gash*

Linda just moved in on Joey. She did everything for Joey. She'd help Joey get into his pants, promise him a blowjob if he'd get in the bathtub, handled all his money. I mean, she fuckin' wiped his ass, you know? She did *everything* for him. Everything. She got herself so intertwined in his life that he could not live, or do anything, without her. She just started doing everything he couldn't do. Because of his problem with obsessive-compulsive disorder he would just come to a standstill sometimes, he couldn't move. Or it would take him so long to do something, twenty times before we could move on to something else. It was just bizarre. I remember we were in this big hurry to get out of the city one time, we had to drive somewhere—and Joey had to touch something. He had to go back in somewhere and he was, like, in a panic. We could not leave until he got to go and touch this thing, or else he was gonna lose it, it was not going to be right until he did that.

I didn't even know this about him, I didn't notice it at first. Johnny would say, "Just watch him sometimes." I really didn't pay that much attention to the other guys. I was just living with Johnny. I didn't really talk to them much after Johnny and I were together. It wasn't until we started hanging out with Joey and Linda that I noticed the things he did.

Johnny told me this story about Joey when I first met him, that Joey had actually been born a Siamese twin and he had an operation to remove the twin at birth, which resulted in its death, and that's where that huge scar that ran across Joey's lower back came from. And that's why he was obsessive-compulsive—because he still had a psychic link to the twin and had to do all those things over for the twin. Weird story, I'm sure Johnny made it up, but how *did* he get that huge scar? [8]

Joey was a really nice guy, I liked him a lot, but wow—he had a really severe case of OCD, I think! But as I say, I never talked much with him. He was very quiet and didn't know what to say to me. Later, when we started hanging out with him and Linda, he sort of loosened up.

The funny thing was that Johnny was kind of obsessive-compulsive, too, but in a totally different way. His was a regimental thing. Joey's was a true obsessive thing, where something would be on his mind and he was at a standstill until he did this stupid little thing which didn't mean anything. Johnny had all these rules because *that's the way he liked it*, that's how he was taught. Going to military school, things had to be just so and he had to keep himself that way. He wanted to be in control of his surroundings. So he put on this fake pressure all the time—that military way he ran things.

> *Johnny Ramone ... was the self-appointed boss of the band and would override the opinion or point of view of anyone else. Nothing could be done without Johnny's approval or consent. ... He would make rules for the whole band professionally and personally, and if you went against him in any way he would make life absolutely miserable for you and treat you like an outcast. ... He was nice to his fans, but he had a whole other side to him that we all experienced and were victims of at one time or another. ... If you strayed from his rules you would pay a dear price, and he made sure of this. It didn't matter who you were.   — Vera Ramone*

Yeah, Johnny and Joey were very different kinds of people. Totally! Joey had a real psychological condition. Johnny just wanted everything done a certain way, like folding the shirts or making a bed. He taught me the way that he wanted everything, and that's the way I did it and that's the *only* way I did it. He was spoiled, he liked everything done his way—which, of course, was "perfect"—being a Libra.

*Joey, do you have any idea what you'd be doing if you weren't the lead singer in a rock and roll band?*
**Joey:** Yeah, I'd be the lead singer in a rock and roll band.
**Johnny:** He'd be selling flowers. ...
*Joey, what were you leaning towards when you started to sing?*
**Joey:** I was leaning to the left.
*The man is downright cryptic.*
**Johnny:** You were a drummer.
*Right. Do you ever feel like you want to do something with your hands when you're up there? Play guitar, perhaps?*
**Johnny:** He's holding on to the mike stand.
**Joey:** I have to do a lot of things with my hands when I'm up there, y' know.
**Dee Dee:** I've seen him slapping kids.
*You guys are nowhere near as mean as your image on-stage.*
**Tommy:** We are as mean as you see us onstage. That's us. We put all our meanness into our music.
**Johnny:** We can be mean sometimes offstage. *—New York Rocker*

**[T]he Ramones used to torture Joey, and Johnny really hated him. ... Really had no**

*tolerance for him. Joey had a lot of problems, physical problems, whatever, and Johnny was not having it. One time, they said, 'What's that smell?' [Joey] had, like, underwear sticking out, he'd been wearing the same underwear for like three tours and it had just decayed, he smelled, and he was weird—Johnny hated that. Hated that. So I think part of the attraction [of Linda] was that he was getting back at the creep."  — Gyda Gash*

I don't think he hated Joey. Why would he hate him? I could see Joey hating Johnny! He didn't have any right to hate Joey. They were best friends for a long time. I mean, not best friends, but they knew each other, like, forever. OK, yeah, maybe they didn't. To be in that sort of situation and have to be around each other—and then have this thing happen, where you can't even talk to each other—yeah, I guess I would hate that person.

⌘

Next night, at a folkie club in San Jose, the Bodega [*February 24, 1977*], there was no chance for any problems to develop. A sign at the door listed all the things that aren't allowed, which

included all leather jackets. They didn't
make the Ramones remove theirs,
although all under-age girl-friends (4
outta 4) had to wait outside the kitchen
door while the boys played. ... But by
far the best Ramones show of their
California trip was at Slick Willy's, a
beer hall on the outskirts of Sacramento
[*March 2*] ... Johnny and Joey could
not keep straight faces when a local
psychotic did a psychedelic kazotsky in
front of the stage. "First guy who's ever
done the blitzkrieg bop right," Dee Dee
told us.

—*New York Rocker*, "Pressed Lips"

I remember that show where we were too young to come into the club,
at least Claudia and I were! That was one of the only times Connie
Gripp came with us and the three of us had to sit in the kitchen while the
Ramones played. But we all got our picture taken later and it ended up
in some rock newspaper, with Connie seen prominently. Mostly us girls
were hidden, until Vera came along and wanted to be more public.

That February 1977 tour was also when we met Phil Spector. Yeah,
that was crazy. We stayed up all night with him, which was OK, Johnny
and I stayed up all night every night. But Johnny didn't like somebody
tellin' him that he can't leave! I think from the start he didn't really like
Phil Spector too much.

After one of the shows at the Whisky, somebody, I don't know if it
was Phil Spector or someone else, threw a big party for the Ramones on
the Santa Monica Pier. That was a great party—they had the whole pier

for *us!* I never hear about this party, but I remember Johnny and I had fun on the merry-go-round. One of Phil Spector's twin bodyguards knocked me down as he jumped off it. It was an accident, and I was OK, but he was so concerned and so sorry, he kept apologizing to me and Johnny.

And then one night we all went out to Phil Spector's house. Everybody wanted to go. Johnny probably didn't want to go to begin with, but felt he had to, to be polite. Other people always wanted to go to a celebrity's house or something like that; Johnny was the only one who didn't care that much, unless it was a baseball player, or Stephen King.

> While **Little Linda** was snooping around during a get together for the **Ramones** at **Phil Spector**'s mansion, the mysterious millionaire informed her that the room she was peeking into was the one in which he threw a birthday party for **Mick Jagger** 8 years ago. Everything was left completely intact, a shrine to one of Spector's idols.
> —*New York Rocker,* "Pressed Lips"

As the night progressed, Phil got weirder. I don't know what he had done, what he was doing, probably speed or coke, but he just didn't wanna be alone. He was at the piano trying to entertain us, playing songs and singing. He seemed like he really wanted to do their album and he was all hyped up, and he was trying to be friendly and charming and entertaining that night. It just got a little out of hand, and Johnny I guess got paranoid when he didn't want us to leave.

And the guns… I think Phil was carrying a gun even when he came to the Whisky and he had his two bodyguards with him, those twin bodyguards [*Dan and David Kessel*].

> When **Phil Spector** saw **Dee Dee Ramone** he knew he had met his match. The do-do so provoked Spector with his whining of "I'm So Happy" that Mr. S. pulled a gun on him. The Ramones happy retort was "Go ahead and shoot me, I won't shoot back.
> —*New York Rocker,* "Pressed Lips"

After that tour, we came back to New York and that's when Johnny and I moved in together, in March. Right after that, I went with him on the Ramones' first tour of Europe, with the Talking Heads [*April–June 1977; tour ended in London June 5-6*]. I had been arrested in New York for public lewdness while I was dancing, and I remember I had to go to court—I went to court in the morning and then I went to the airport and flew to London. Some guys from Television were on the same flight, Richard Lloyd and some other guys. Not Tom Verlaine, though. [*Television's debut album* Marquee Moon *had been released February 8, 1977.*] Johnny was already in Europe, so I travelled with Claudia.

That was a great trip! It was great over there, everyone was really into the punk phenomenon going on. It was fun meeting all the bands I was listening to. In England the punk scene was all over the country, not just in cities like New York and L.A. Everyone was going punk. And I remember the Newcastle brown ale and barley wine! We bought a lot of English records. And we ran into my old boyfriend Richard Rockwood in London. Johnny told me to tell him to stay away if he didn't want any trouble. Richard didn't want to get beat up, so he stayed away.

I think it was on this trip, in Amsterdam one night, that some members of the local Hell's Angels decided they didn't want the show to end, so they busted in the door of the dressing room. None of the "brudders" were too brave right then, not even Dee Dee with his knives. The Hell's Angels just wanted to be friendly and let the guys know how much they appreciated the music, but they were a little intimidating, to say the least.

The Ramones had a pretty good relationship with the Talking Heads, so that made the traveling easier. They were totally different from the Ramones, that's for sure—they were like intellectuals or something, compared with other bands! They mainly read books on the bus, they had brought boxes of books along with them. Very smart people. Jerry Harrison, if you asked him any question, he would sit down and go on and on for hours about whatever it was. But we didn't socialize with them, really; I think Johnny and I went out to dinner with David Byrne maybe one night. Otherwise, we didn't mingle with them too much except on the bus, when one of them would come over to talk. Usually Jerry Harrison.

*[T]here's this ancient story about Johnny and me and the Talking Heads. They were auditioning at CBGB, and Johnny and I were there to talk to Hilly [Kristal, the owner] about an opening act for the Ramones on the coming weekend. And Hilly said, "Wait*

*a minute fellas, I want you to hear this band
that's going to audition right now. They just
drove down from Providence. They're kind
of weird to me...the bass player's a woman,
and...well, you should hear them." Johnny
was very critical of anyone who might open
for the Ramones, and anyone the Ramones
would open for. The Talking Heads had
played for about ten seconds and Johnny
said to me, "They suck...it's fine...they can
open for us." Ironically, the Talking Heads
went on to sell lots more records...than the
Ramones ever did.  — Danny Fields*

When Johnny liked a band and felt they weren't too much
competition, like totally different than the Ramones, he would be very
nice to them and book them to play with the Ramones a lot. Like in
particular, Suicide. I told Johnny about them because I was friends with
Martin [*Rev*] and Alan [*Vega*]. Martin was fucking my old roommate
Elida Ramirez and that's how I met them. When Johnny heard that they
didn't have much of an audience and got booed offstage and stuff thrown
at them, he wanted them to play with the Ramones! He never listened
to their music, even when I told him [*the Suicide song*] "Johnny" had
been written about him. All he cared about was that they wouldn't be any
competition for him.

But they got along pretty well with the Talking Heads. Except for
when Johnny would start acting up and fighting with me. Tina Weymouth
didn't like that at all. She finally said to I think Linda Stein [*Ramones
co-manager, with Danny Fields*] that she couldn't stand the way Johnny

treated me, and if he hit me one more time they were going to leave
the tour, so Linda came and spoke to Johnny. Linda Stein was nice to
me. She wanted all of us to make millions. I think she wanted to be a
manager so perhaps she'd get laid by the bands, ha! [9]

Another thing I remember about that tour is going to Stonehenge.
Johnny was pissed off that we drove all those extra hours and feigned
that he didn't want to be there, but actually we talked a lot about it later,
how magical and mystical it seemed. We felt a strange energy there and
we talked about Druids and black sacrifices and witches. I know Monte's
book [*On the Road with the Ramones*] says Johnny refused to get off the
tour bus and see it, but we did, we got out and took pictures. We loved
it—he brought it up a lot for the rest of the tour.

That was a really good tour because you could feel the Ramones
picking up momentum, definitely. The shows started selling out
everywhere and that would make Johnny happy. He wanted all the shows
to be sold out, and they usually were, from pretty early on, I would say.

# 1978

*Did Roxy ever talk about the rumor that she had been murdered? This was a really weird thing. A rumor went around CBGB's one night that Roxy had been killed and everyone was very upset. I went through my diaries and it is so interesting that the date for the "Roxy is dead" myth was Friday the 13th of January 1978. This night Suicide played at Max's and there was a great jam session with many musicians including Ivan Kral, David Johansen, Ivan Julian, Syl Sylvain, and Walter Lure. So Max's was packed that night and everyone must have heard Roxy was "dead." In fact, I wrote in my diary that she was 'murdered' and that Cheryl Revenge called me the next day to talk about it and we were "freaked out and paranoid". Then Roxy just showed up and she was fine!* — Eileen Polk

The mystery of **Roxy's** murder still prevails. She was always a playful object of my poison pen but death was surely an unwarranted horror. My sympathies to **Johnny Ramone.**

— *New York Rocker,* "Pressed Lips"

NICE OF JANIS TO SEND HER sympathies, huh? The mystery of
Roxy's death. That was weird. Danny Fields called Johnny one night
when we were out on tour and got around to asking him if I was with
him, or if he knew where I was. He didn't want to blurt anything out in
case it was true. Finally, after John said I was right there with him, he
told him what people were saying. It was a mistaken identity, someone
else, but I remember Bleecker Bob, every time we saw him afterwards,
he would always say, "Roxy! I thought you were dead!" False alarm, but
it gave me the creeps.

⌘

In 1978 Tommy decided to leave the band, and Johnny was thinking
about who should replace him. He asked me, "What about Marc Bell?"
I was surprised he even brought his name up. I didn't want to suggest
Marc because I figured if I did, forget about it, Johnny wouldn't want
him in the band! Then he mentioned Marc, and of course I agreed with
his choice. I said I thought he'd be great, but I didn't want to seem *too*
enthusiastic so that John wouldn't get jealous. So Marc joined as Marky
Ramone in June 1978. I didn't think Johnny liked Marc. I guess it didn't
matter whether he liked him or not, he thought he was a good drummer.

But actually, there was never a problem between Johnny and Marc. I
think Johnny respected Marc because he was a good musician. And Marc
had moved out once I started seeing Johnny, so they didn't get into any
sort of anything.

Marc fit in perfectly with them. Marion was always with him and
she had a good stabilizing effect on him. He was a big drinker when

I was with him (*which later got him thrown out of the Ramones, in December 1982*), but he got sober eventually (*and re-joined the band in 1987*).

That was also the year Dee Dee and Vera were married, on September 2. But we didn't go to the wedding, nooo! Johnny didn't want to go. He and Dee Dee weren't particularly getting along at the time, and he didn't like Vera. Even though she was sort of straight, he didn't like her. He thought she was empty-headed. He used to call her "the Turtle"—you know the turtle in the Bugs Bunny cartoons? That's what he said she reminded him of. He would make fun of them trying to be bourgeois with the money crap and "Dee Dee and Baby Doll." Johnny hated all that and hated them. Funny, he was *so* opposed to that kind of lifestyle when they did it, but he seemed to embrace it later on in L.A., with Linda.

Personally, I had no problem with Vera. She was closer with Linda at the time but later, after the Ramones, she was the only one who stayed in touch with me. She was kind to me, we spoke on the phone a lot and she even wrote to me in prison. We're still close, she's been a good friend to me and I'm very grateful for her friendship.

Anyway, we didn't go to the wedding. I don't *think* he went, ha ha ha!—I don't know, did he go without me?

⌘

The Ramones were in California again at the end of 1978, and in December they filmed the movie, *Rock n Roll High School*. I was here for the whole thing, I was on the set with them almost every day. It was sort of fun, making a movie, and it was funny watching them try to act.

They actually had a lot of lines in the original script, but as time went on they kept cutting out the lines because they couldn't say them. Dee Dee was reduced to, I think, one line in the whole movie. I think he just had to say "pizza" or something like that, and they had to do a bunch of takes to get that right.

Johnny had lines, too—he had cool lines, and he said them all right. He seemed to have fun doing the movie and he liked the actors who were in it. Dick Miller he liked a lot, and Grady Sutton, who had been in W.C. Fields movies. And Mary Woronov and Paul Bartel, we liked them. Mary Woronov had been a Warhol superstar but I didn't know her, never crossed paths with her at Max's—that was before my time, the Warhol crowd at Max's, and Johnny didn't hang out with any of them either, ever. We went to PJ Soles's house for dinner, she was married to Dennis Quaid at the time. And Alan Arkush, the director, was a big fan. It was between the Ramones and Cheap Trick, I think, who would be in the movie and he wanted the Ramones, so that's how they got the job. He was a cool guy. We'd go over to his place and watch movies. He was very friendly.

For Johnny being such a movie fan, to be in a movie was somethin' else. Even when I first moved out here in 1990 and I was doing extra work in movies, he was excited about that, too. He would ask me every night, "Where you going to be working tomorrow? Who are you going to be working with? Oh, take your book, I know you got a book that he wrote, you should take it with you and have him sign it." He was really excited for me to be here.

But as far as *Rock n Roll High School*, I don't know if he was *proud* of it...I guess he was. It was an okay film for what it was, there were some good people in it, but it was kind of silly. It's not the kind of movie he'd want to see if he wasn't in it. But it went on to become a cult classic, and I'm sure he loved it for that reason.

When it came out, though, he was afraid that nobody was going to go see it. [Rock n Roll High School *was released in April 1979*]. So every night, we'd walk over to the Eighth Street Playhouse and sit in the back because he wanted to see how many people showed up! Every night. On the weekends, when they had the midnight movies, we got to see those for free. One time they had *The Rocky Horror Picture Show*, which he'd never seen—all the horror films that we saw, he'd never seen that. I said, "Well, we should stay and see it!" So we stayed, and as soon as they started coming down the aisle with the gold panties on and the toilet paper, he just wanted to get out of there! He was afraid he was going to get hit with something or catch some disease, so we had to leave.

That was only the second time we ever walked out of a movie. The other time was *The Last House on Dead-End Street*, in Times Square [*limited release, 1977*]. They were killing cows with that big gun that slams a bolt into their heads. That was like the first scene in the movie and he walked out, he couldn't stand it. He was an animal lover, although he didn't admit it. Plus we were sitting right up front in the first row because the theatre was packed, those were the only seats, and it was mainly black people around us yelling at the screen, so he got upset and we left. It was my fault, of course, because I picked the movie.

# 1979

*"Baby, I Love You" is a black mark that will never go away. When we started I said, "Oh Phil, we should do one of your songs." I was all for doing one of his songs. I thought we'd just play one of his songs! Then I had to leave. My father died. I didn't play on it. Mark and Joey were huge Phil Spector fans and what he was doing that was rotten, they didn't care. Dee Dee hated him. Dee Dee stayed a punk throughout.* —Johnny Ramone

JOHNNY'S FATHER DIED WHILE they were out in California making the record with Phil Spector—*End of the Century* [*May 5, 1979*]. I remember he showed up at home, out of the blue, very upset. Very upset. He said he had to get to Florida. I didn't know that his father had died, and something had happened to me, too, I was in a crisis. I had gotten raped by a group of guys in a band. They kidnapped me to New Jersey and dumped me by the side of the road. So it was like the day after this happened, and all of a sudden Johnny came flying in. I didn't know about his father and I started telling him what had happened to me. I was sort of hysterical, it was quite an ordeal. But he wasn't feeling very sympathetic. He blamed me for it, and he got so pissed off at what I was telling him that he beat the crap outta me. He was having problems with Phil Spector, too, so I think he was taking out his frustration and anger. But it was really fucked-up. He beat me silly and flew to Florida by himself, then back to L.A. to finish his album.

> *[Monte] came to meet me at the airport with Linda when my father died. We were doing the Phil Spector album and she insisted on coming to the airport, too. I thought, "Wow, this girl is really nice to me." From that point on, I knew. I must have been in a vulnerable mood because my father had died.*
>
> *— Johnny Ramone*

I didn't go to California with him—I guess I wanted to stay home. I had no idea there was anything between him and Linda at that time, and I don't really believe there was. We weren't even hanging out with Joey and Linda then. I never knew she went with Monte to the airport to pick John up after his father died. Not until I read in Monte's book, years later. I do remember he sort of hinted at a threesome with Linda once, and I told him she was too ugly and stupid, and that it would have to be someone more like Anya, or Gyda, or my sister.

⌘

After I started seeing Johnny, I didn't see much of any of my friends anymore. Johnny was so protective and dominating over me, he didn't even want me speaking with anyone. Then Linda asked Johnny if it was OK if she talked to me because she saw no one else was allowed to. Well, she is the one person I *didn't* want to talk to. So that's how she and John got chummy. I actually pushed the two of them together because Joey didn't like walking to the store and shit like that, and neither did I. So the two of them went waiting on us. That was a mistake.

She became friends with me, and she was supposed to be my "best friend" and everything. She would call me constantly, all day long, every day. She didn't have anybody to hang out with, either. After a while I started believing, *Oh, she's OK.* I thought we were getting to know each other, and I thought maybe she might be a person underneath all this.

Yeah, it was fun at first, you know? And it was fun when Johnny and I started socializing with Joey and Linda. All of a sudden we could go out and go over to Joey's, and there were people to talk to. At least it was somebody for me to talk to. Pretty soon the four of us were constantly together, constantly. We lived on 10th Street between Third and Fourth Avenues and they lived at 9th and Third, right on the corner. So we were right near each other and if we weren't on the phone, we were at each other's house or doing something together. It was like I couldn't shake 'em.

She fooled me, pretending to be my best friend. She weaseled her way into our lives and she fooled me into believing that she was a friend to me, that she cared about me. That's the way it went. Before this, she had latched on to Vera. It was the same thing with Vera and Dee Dee, constantly being together.

I encouraged Johnny to hang out with Linda because he had no friends. And I didn't think she would be any problem for me—I never dreamed that Johnny would have any interest other than being a friend, you know? Because she was a *dog*, ha ha ha! And stupid! I mean, Johnny always told me he really liked that I was intelligent. He respected my opinion and he would always ask me about everything. We were close. I gave him a lot of advice!

But I was sort of shut off and I was alone a lot. And he would want me to go and do things with him all the time, "Let's go to the store and get some stuff." Well, I wouldn't always want to. So when he became friends with Linda, it took a little bit of the pressure off me. He didn't have to drag me here and there. She was always ready to jump up and do anything. *She'll* go with him. Good, fine. Then I don't have to go. So the two of them would go run errands and Joey and I would stay home and relax. Joey didn't want to walk to the store, that's for sure! It would've been an all-night project!

I gave Johnny plenty of room and let him have some freedom, whatever he wanted. Remember, master/slave fantasy. I can be terribly jealous, but he had never given me cause to worry. I was confident, I didn't feel like I needed to be there watching over him all the time, like Vera with Dee Dee. And Linda? Please. She was everything he despised. I thought.

*The Rattlers were playing with the Ramones that July 1979 at the Diplomat Hotel in Manhattan when Monte made a cryptic comment to me.*

*"Something's going on," Monte murmured at the show. 'Something's weird with John and Linda."*

*"Whaddaya mean?" I asked him.*

*"You haven't heard anything?" Monte asked.*

*"Heard what?" I answered.*

*"Never mind," Monte said, dropping the subject.*

*I assumed he was talking about something silly, like Johnny telling Linda not to talk in the van or something. I dropped it, as well.*

*— Mickey Leigh*

*We played with the Ramones at the Second Chance in Ann Arbor at one point [probably March 8, 1978]. A couple days later [April 4–5] they were doing a show in Toronto, and the opener canceled and the promoter called and said, "Do you want to open for the Ramones?" Yes we did. After the show Johnny Ramone came up and introduced himself. And, well, he really pursued me after that. A year later, after [the album] End of the Century [came out], Johnny called and said, "This is where we're playing. What shows do you want to open?" They were playing a venue on the west side, but I didn't really want to go because the promoter, Gail Parenteau, did not like me. She thought that I was going after all of the guys she was after. Johnny just said, "We'll put you on the guest list and make sure you get in." And I'm, like, it's just going to be a hassle you know. And then he said, "We won't play if you don't get in." "Oh, I am there." You know I want to be there for that conversation. After that Johnny used to call me every day from the road. It was really uncomfortable when I would go see Johnny on*

*the road. Years later I realized that the reason*
*everything was so uncomfortable was because*
*he was going out with Linda. And not only was he*
*going out with Linda, but he was having me come*
*to shows and used my band to open shows.*

*When I saw [the documentary] End of the*
*Century, I figured out the dates and I went, "Oh*
*my god, like, okay. No wonder everybody hated*
*me." I still have letters and cards from him.*
— *Nikki Corvette, singer, Nikki and the Corvettes.*

# 1980

*Each day of our European adventure we witnessed the friendship of John and Linda getting stronger and stronger. Even though Roxy was also with John on the road, and Linda was Joey's girlfriend, it was obvious to everyone that there was something going on between John and Linda. John was not particularly friendly with Joey, but he and Linda were becoming chummier with every passing day. By the time we were in Belgium [February 12], they were coordinating their outfits! One morning, as everyone was piling into the smelly old bus to drive to Milan, Italy, we all noticed that Linda and Johnny were wearing matching peach-colored sweatshirts. John never dressed like this before, and it was clear that Linda's sense of style was rubbing off on him. I could see the anguish in Joey's eyes, he was helpless against John. Linda was slowly succumbing to John's controlling ways and there was nothing Joey or anybody else could do about it.  — Vera Ramone*

IN JANUARY 1980 THE RAMONES went to Europe again—England,

the Netherlands, Belgium, Italy, Paris and London. I was pregnant on that tour.

At first, I didn't know. It took me by surprise because I didn't think I could get pregnant. I was already 23 and it hadn't happened. We never used any sort of birth control or anything and I never got pregnant. Then I got pregnant twice that year, one right after the other. We started being a little careful after that!

We were in Europe the first time and I remember crossing the English Channel on a ferry and I was sick and smells made me sick. All I wanted was mashed potatoes and milk. By the time we got back to New York and I went for the abortion it was like 90 days, they said if it had been one more day they wouldn't have been able to do it. [*First abortion probably late February 1980.*] I felt empty afterwards. I remember Johnny put his hand on my stomach and said, "No more baby!"

The second time was only a month or two later and we were at home, so I didn't have any problem getting to a doctor that time, I could take care of it right away [*probably mid-April*]. Johnny took me to the place and I remember it was on the highest floor of the building, maybe the 12th floor or something. When it was over and I was about to leave, there was a power failure. The elevators were out, so I had to walk down the stairs. And you're not feelin' real well after an abortion, you know? I was a little messed up, a little shaky, and I had to walk down all these flights of stairs in the dark. When I got all the way down to the ground floor, there's Johnny standing there. He wouldn't walk up to me—he waited at the bottom of the stairs for me to come down! But at least he came to pick me up.

He was adamant that he did not want children, and I don't see how we could have done it at the time. For one thing, I didn't think I needed to get married and have babies to be validated as a woman. And a baby would not have fit in with our lifestyle, he was out of town so much and I was out with him. I don't think that would have been a very good life for a kid. And I didn't want to take care of babies then. What am I gonna do, stay at home with a baby? And miss all the fun? No, none of the girls got to have children.

So I was in no hurry to get married or have kids. But I guess I should have, now that I look back on it! I think I was frightened by the whole thing, it was scary for me to even think about. It just frightened me for some reason. I didn't know if I could handle people. It scares me even now, like, how do you *do* that? I have no idea.

I figured we had plenty of time in the future. I was just in my early twenties, John was in his early thirties, and we were so much in love.

Yeah, children. I'm sure Johnny would have been a good father, if we'd had a kid. But he insisted that he hated children, and his mother insisted that *she* hated children, too. I remember right after I had the second abortion, the Ramones played in Chicago for a week and Johnny's mother Stella came up [*mid-May 1980*]. My mother, being the ever-gracious lady that she was, escorted her around town in her convertible El Dorado. We took her shopping at Water Tower Place and then I made a stop at the doctor's office to pick up a diaphragm. It was a gynecologist's office, and there were pictures of babies on the wall. Stella looked around and she said, "Oh! Babies. I hate babies!" And my mother said, "I'm sure you did *not* hate John when he was a baby!" Ha ha ha! And she says, "Well, no, no, no." She didn't hate babies, she just didn't want John to have any children at that time!

But it was bizarre! "I hate babies"—I've never heard a woman say that who's a mother!

Johnny didn't want kids, but he did love animals, especially Little, our blind calico cat that I brought home one night. At first he said I couldn't keep her; she used to push the closet door so it shook and made a noise, and he was a very light sleeper. But then after I realized she was blind, he fell in love with her. He treasured that cat and worried over her, took her to the hospital whenever she was sick. He probably had her 20 years.

⌘

Johnny really didn't like being around the other guys in the band, so he was upset a lot on tour. He didn't want to socialize with them and never did. And I spent so much time sitting and reading, or pretending to be reading so that nobody would talk to me, that the people around the band didn't even know me! They'd swear I wasn't even there. The only time I got to relax was in the room, when we were away from everybody else.

It was stressful, those long tours. They weren't *bad* times, of course, and I know it was pretty much the "height" of punk, but for me it didn't seem all that exciting. It was more like drudgery! Like seven years of hell that never stopped. It was not a lot of fun for me. We were never at home, I was living out of a suitcase, traveling around, carrying suitcases every day, a different place all the time…We had no home life. We had nothing, we lived in one room. And he would watch me every second. I couldn't smoke a cigarette, he watched how much alcohol I consumed—everything. Then he started having to go with me when I bought my clothes. It was just ridiculous.

I swear, you look at pictures of us—if there *are* any pictures—we were always alone. Just me and him with our books, reading, by ourselves. We stayed away from everybody. Like that one picture in Monte's book of the two of us, sitting on the train in Japan, by ourselves. And we both have that look on our faces like, "Why are you bothering us?" Well, *I'm* smiling—*he* looks pissed off because somebody was taking a picture of us. He didn't want anybody taking pictures of us, because then his mother might see me with him, his father might see me with him, his *wife* might see me with him…he didn't want *anybody* to see me with him.

We led a very insular life, not only because of his rivalry with and jealousy of other bands, but because of his insecurity about my alcohol abuse. He kept me away from others, and in doing so kept himself away, too. He felt that my "friends" just wanted to party with me and get me high and get me into trouble. I admit that I was bad when I'd get drunk, but it came out of his tyranny, really, that I got that way. It was the only way out of my shell.

After a while with him, my personality was gone. I couldn't be myself. I couldn't even voice an opinion. Before this, you couldn't keep my mouth shut! Nobody told me what to do, I had all sorts of boyfriends, I was always out, I was just crazy. Then all of a sudden I'm this quiet, shy girl who does whatever this guy says. I felt invisible, unnecessary and useless hanging around him, not doing anything myself and not having anything to say because he was watching my every move and listening to everything I'd say—even a smile. I was afraid to say anything in case it would be the wrong thing. He criticized me whenever I did make comments. He would call me names or say, "No one wants to hear what you have to say." He needed a punching bag. The only time I spoke was when we were alone, otherwise I had my head stuck in a book, always. I was like a trophy being carted around on his arm. I couldn't do anything! I couldn't do *anything*.

*In the beginning, it was all about Frederick's of Hollywood and Paradise Bootery and stockings and a lot of S&M gear, rubber clothes. She had money, she'd always get the greatest fashions from London. But then we started morphing into the '80s, God, that was a horrible time—the fuckin New Romantic poufy clothes and pastels and all that shit—*

*and the hair got big, and things got weird*
*and punk rock wasn't making any money.*
*That's when he started becoming really, really*
*obsessively controlling and he would pick out*
*her clothes. But I think it was part of their*
*game also. And he started to get more and*
*more grumpy. More and more intolerant as*
*time went on.  — Gyda Gash*

And it was like he couldn't do anything without *me*, either. He couldn't bear to go anywhere without me. If I wasn't there with him, he would be on the telephone calling me, calling me, constantly, constantly. It was like I was a possession of his and he didn't need anybody else. He slowly cut me off from everybody, even from my sister Carolyn. I remember he threw her out of the apartment once. She was really beautiful, really pretty, and she would come and stay with us a couple times a year. Well, this one time he got pissed off at her because she was hanging out with Adam Ant. Adam and the Ants were in town and Carolyn had met Adam in Chicago, we both partied with them in Chicago, and then she came out to New York to party with him there, too.

I don't know if Johnny was jealous or what, but he got so angry with her over Adam Ant that he took her suitcases and threw them out in the hallway and told her to get the hell out, go back to your boyfriend. And as she was walkin' out the door, he kicked her! Yeah. Kicked her in the ass and threw her out of the house. Then she grabbed me and was trying to pull me out, too—"I'm takin' her with me!"

She and Johnny didn't get along, ha ha ha! They really didn't. Carolyn was very thin and gorgeous and would always stick up for me when Johnny would start yelling or beating on me. She would fight back.

I would fight back, too, but I wasn't any good at it. Other times they seemed to get along OK. She could be good sometimes. But when she was around him, she'd try to act like I was the fucked-up one and she was there to take care of me or something. She put on this act around him like she was the big girl. And she wasn't. She was very spoiled and very young. I used to dress her up so she looked much more mature than her age, which was 14, 15 back then. Very beautiful, but she would put on this front like she knew it all when inside she was a scared little girl. Our father died when she was ten and she never got over it. She looked like Marilyn Monroe and was obsessed with death. That was Carolyn. She's dead now—she died of an overdose when she was twenty-two.

⌘

What I remember most about 1980 was going to Japan [*June 27–July 4, 1980*]. That was fun! I liked Japan a lot. We had a good time there, Johnny liked the Japanese and it was cool. The food was good, the people were nice, the hotels were nice and it was very clean and very high-tech. We liked it. And the Ramones went over very well, all the shows were packed. They had a good time in Japan.

That's when Linda really started coming around me, and we started hanging out with her and Joey all the time. Before that, she had been best friends with Vera.

Vera really liked Linda and they were inseparable for a while, did everything together. But I think Linda actually envied her, because when she was hanging out with Vera and Dee Dee, she had Joey buy her a diamond, which she touted as her engagement ring, and told everyone she and Joey would be married soon, too.

And then one day Linda just stopped talking to Vera, and she and Joey started hanging around with me and Johnny instead. Linda just totally snubbed her so bad. She wouldn't even talk to her anymore! I could see Vera was practically in tears, she was so upset. She kept going up to Linda, asking, "Why won't you talk to me? What did I do?" I couldn't believe Linda would do something like that. But she didn't care! She was vicious. She chewed Vera up and spit her out, kicked her to the curb, just because Johnny and I didn't hang with them. Looking back on it, she was after Johnny, wanted to be with Johnny, and she was going to do anything she had to do to get to Johnny.

After Japan, the tour went to Australia and then to New Zealand. I remember the zoo in Sydney, that was a lot of fun—I got to hold a koala bear and take pictures with the koala bears, and we got to pet and feed the kangaroos. We always liked going to zoos. Johnny liked animals and so did I, I love animals, so whenever we were around a zoo, we'd go if we had the chance.

And we went bowling! I had not gone bowling since I was about 14. We all went bowling one night, me and Johnny and Joey and Linda. It was really fun.

But in Australia I got an ear infection that threw my balance off so that I felt like I was moving all the time. It was really bad. I don't think I went to any of the shows in Australia, I think I stayed in every night. I wanted to go but I was just too sick. Getting home was torture. We flew to Hawaii, then from Hawaii to Los Angeles, then we had to get off the plane and take a taxi to Los Tacos (*Ramones' favorite Mexican fast food restaurant, in West Hollywood*)—which I don't even eat!—take a taxi back, get back on the plane, and fly from Los Angeles to New York. I was so sick by the time we got back to New York [*end of July 1980*]. I was all screwed up. They had to go to Europe pretty much right away, but I didn't want to go. Johnny didn't want me flying with an ear infection, and I didn't want anybody to see me except my mother, so I went to Chicago and stayed at my mother's to try and recuperate.

I didn't get over that for a long time—I was really sick for like a year. I couldn't go out touring anymore, I just couldn't. Johnny went to Europe in August and he was going to send me a ticket but I really didn't want to go. I needed some time off, so I said, "Look, I'll meet you there, just send me a ticket later and I'll come out."

But I didn't. I didn't go at all. First I had the ear thing, then I had to have a nose operation in New York to fix a deviated septum. I was in the hospital for a couple of days with that, because my nose had to be "set" for a day or two, it was all stuffed with gauze. My mother came to New York to be with me. I remember Joey sent me a card, it was really cool. He drew all these funny little drawings on it, guys excavating my nose and funny little things.

For the record, the deviated septum was not from drug use! I never did cocaine back in those days at all, when everybody was doing it. I wasn't doing any drugs at that time. It was all that flying and having the ear infection and then a sinus infection, somehow it messed up my nose, too.

One day during all this, Johnny called me from Europe and he was complaining that Joey and Linda were being assholes to him, that they weren't talking to him. He was saying, "You gotta get here, you gotta get over here right away—she's not talking to me!" I said, Who's not talking to you? "Y'know—*her!* Her!" And he was talking about Linda.

He would call me up and say, "She won't talk to me, she's being mean to me, she's giving me all this shit." He probably became dependent on her for her stupid remarks or whatever, her "friendship," when I started not being around so much. But it didn't make sense to me. I thought she was my friend, so I was calling her up and saying, "What kind of shit are you giving Johnny? He said that you're being mean to him and you won't talk to him," and I'm thinking everything's fine. Can you imagine? I was calling her and yelling at her and shit, and it was all nonsense games. Just games.

She wasn't in love with him! She just liked that he would do stupid little antics, like throwing things around her, and she would bend over wearing these short skirts right in front of him. She did that all the time until I was ready to kill her. Acting stupid like that in front of him all the time. He just thought she was *so cute*, and he became so infatuated with her stupidity. He was blinded by it! He'd never been around somebody like that, I guess. She was really annoying.

Nobody in the band liked her. Nobody really liked her. When this all started happening, everybody saw it before I did. I thought something was going on, but I didn't want to discuss it—it couldn't be happening, because that couldn't happen to *me*, you know?

*The first time we kissed, we were in a cab... going to our accountant Ira Herzog's office in the summer of 1980. Me and Linda were the only ones who knew.  — Johnny Ramone*

Meanwhile, this girl would go out behind Joey's back and *spend*. She was in charge of all the money, because Joey couldn't get to the bank too well with his OCD and all, it took him a long time to do anything. So he let her be in charge of running errands. And she would run all his errands, like taking his money to the bank—by way of Fiorucci or Patricia Fields. She'd hide all her purchases from Joey, but she loved putting it out there, how she was in charge of the money.

She went shopping every day and I would go shopping with her.

She'd call me on the phone—"Roxy, can you go shopping with me?" If
Johnny was around we would both go with her. And she'd say, "Oh, if
there's something you want, I'll buy it for you!" And Johnny said no, he
wouldn't like that, but she would insist on buying me things—things *he*
wouldn't like! Or try to front me money to buy clothes, to get Johnny
mad at me. I remember one Christmas she bought me some records that
he told me he didn't want me listening to. He didn't allow me to have
Sex Pistols or Clash albums. I liked them, but Johnny wouldn't let them
in the house. That was his competition and he was jealous, and he didn't
want me to give them business, buying the records.

So Linda bought them for me. It was one Sex Pistols and a couple of
Clash albums that I wanted—*Sandanista!* and some others. She bought
them for me, wrapped them up and gave them to me for Christmas. We
went over to Joey's place and she gave me these gifts, I opened them
up and there they were—these records Johnny didn't want me to have. I
could see by the look on his face that he didn't like it. And she's happy,
smirking, 'cause she knows she's making him upset, and he's upset with
*me*, right? She's laughing about it and what could I say, I can't accept
these? I took them, and when we got home later on I think I put one on.
He walked into the room and picked them up and smashed them all.

And that was the end of that! At that time, he thought The Clash
were better than him, but he didn't want to say that—that they might be
better than the Ramones, or more popular—so they weren't allowed in
the house. That's how he could make them not exist and disappear. Just
destroy them. When I saw the documentary *End of the Century*, where he
says that he thought the Clash were their only real competition, I thought
about him breaking those records!

And yet he would always talk about how those guys came out to meet
them the first time the Ramones played in London (*July 4–5, 1976*) and
how they said they had all started bands because they were so inspired by
the Ramones. That made him happy, made him proud, especially being

older than that bunch. He was already 27 at that time, and they were all around 20. So he liked that they looked up to him, and that he was sort of like a father figure to the English punks bands.

It was the same with the fans, even though a lot of them were crazy, like Boris and Doris. They were their number one fans. They used to come on tour with us, they even came to England with us once. The band used them to sell T-shirts and run errands and do whatever. They had all these misfits that were their biggest fans, a bunch of misfits who would do anything for them! Joey used them a lot 'cause they really would do *anything* for him. Johnny just tried to stay away from them.

And there were all these little girls who used to come see him, too. They used to come to our place, and I would talk to them because they were nice, you know? It's funny, this morning I got a message on Facebook from some girl, talking about this woman who had a taxi, her and her daughter, and I didn't know what she was talking about. Then I remembered this girl and her mother, who used to own a taxi service. Joey knew these people and he would use their taxi once in a while. This girl was in love with Johnny, and she reminded me that she came over to our apartment on 10th Street one time on Johnny's birthday, she and her mother, to deliver a birthday cake. She said she was 12 at the time.

I was always very nice to those little girls who would come over and want to talk to Johnny. I was nice to them and he was nice to them, too. These were *little girls*, and they all thought it was so cool to meet Johnny or his girlfriend and see where he lived. Sometimes I would even invite them in. I would sit and talk to them and they'd tell me their little problems, their boyfriends and whatever. I was lonely, too, so I would talk to these little girls. I know that Linda would never have let them in the house—she hated these girls, hated them. But I tried to be nice to his fans, like he wanted me to be.

*I got this card the other day...from some little girl—she was 11 and her friend was 13 and we were the first rock show she'd ever seen. It made me feel great! Like they're gettin' the right education. They could easily have gone to see REO Speedwagon—or Journey or Toto or somethin'. — Johnny Ramone*

The Ramones really appreciated the people who were that devoted to them. And Johnny also enjoyed being a fan. He was a big rock fan when he was a teenager, and later, when we were together, he would go to the collector's shows and conventions and stand in line to get movie stars' and baseball players' autographs. He didn't mind doing it. So that's I guess why he would stop and talk to fans and would sign anything for them, because he enjoyed doing that himself.

*John was always way ahead of his time. He wasn't biased about music, he'd give anything a chance. But he had his tastes. He liked outrageous, loud, raunchy rock music. ... [He'd] been to see the Yardbirds at the Anderson Theater and the first Rolling Stones concert at the Academy of Music. He'd thrown rocks at the Beatles when they played Shea Stadium. John also liked Ted Nugent, the MC5 and Black Sabbath. ... We both loved Jimi Hendrix. John saw him play at the Cafe Wha back in 1966 or 1967. — Dee Dee Ramone*

*I was a fan like everybody was a fan. ... I would just go with my friends and watch the show. I would be going to all concerts, I'd be trying to see all the concerts I could. I saw the Stones like five times with Brian Jones; I've seen the Who ten times; the Doors probably seven, eight times. Every band. I don't know if there's anybody I didn't see. — Johnny Ramone*

# 1981

EVEN THOUGH THEY WERE his "competition," sometimes we would go out and see other bands. We went to see Public Image Ltd at the Ritz, the famous show when they played behind a screen and the audience rioted [*May 15, 1981*]. Actually, it wasn't so much a riot as a synchronicity—everyone had the same thought at the same time and just started throwing their beer bottles at the screen, and there was a mad dash to the bar to buy more beer to throw! They were bombarding the band with bottles, everybody at the same time, trying to break down that screen. They finally had to shut the place down.

After the breakup of the Sex Pistols in January 1977, singer John Lydon (Johnny Rotten) went on to form Public Image Ltd (PiL). The new group took an anti-punk stance, referring to themselves as a corporation and downplaying their individual identities and contributions. "Part of the impetus behind PiL's posing as a corporation," writes critic Simon Reynolds, "was to ... [suggest] that money making was a potentially subversive strategy of working from within, a stealth campaign that was less spectacular than the Pistols' revolt but more insidious. It was also more honest and less starry-eyed to present rock bands as the money-making enterprises they really were". [1]

Bow Wow Wow was originally scheduled to play the Ritz date but cancelled at the last minute, so Lydon and guitarist Keith Levene, who were living in New York at the time, were brought in as a replacement. Bassist Jeannette Lee and drummer Sam Ulano rounded out the non-band for this show. Located at 125 East 11th St. (currently the nightclub Webster Hall), the Ritz was equipped with high-end video gear, so in keeping with the anti-music concept—and because they had not performed live in some time—PiL chose to stage an experimental "video performance." The idea was that they would play behind a large projection screen, lighted so that their silhouettes appeared on the screen from the back at the same time as Super-8 footage of the band was projected from the front. [2]

The audience (which had been kept outside the venue in pouring rain until showtime) had no idea that this was the plan, so when the music started and the screen did not go up, they began throwing bottles at it. Lydon then proceeded to taunt and insult the crowd; they responded by trying to physically tear down the stage set. Finally, after about 20 minutes of mayhem, the management of the Ritz stopped the performance

Iggy Pop was at that show, too, we saw him there. He seemed really high or something. Loaded. Johnny stuck his hand out to shake his hand,

and Iggy grabbed Johnny's hand like he was going to shake it, then he pulled it and he bit Johnny's thumb really hard! Nobody expected that, but you sort of did from Iggy! It was a fucked-up thing to do if you knew Johnny at all and how he would react. He was really pissed off. You could see on his face, he didn't know what to do! I just wanted to laugh, Gyda wanted to laugh, but this blast of anger—he was, like, appalled at the whole thing and wanted to get away from Iggy. And as we're walkin' away, he's like, *"What an asshole! That guy's a fuckin' asshole!"* We were just trying not to laugh. I didn't need his wrath coming down on me.

Johnny Rotten, John Lydon, wanted to talk to Johnny that night. We must have seen him there but we didn't stay, we went back to our place afterwards. Gyda was with us and I think Howie Pyro, too, he was hanging out with us then. Howie was in a band called the Blessed with Eileen Polk. Gyda started bringing him over and I was trying to get Johnny to cultivate some friends, so Johnny became friendly with him. We were sort of a foursome, because Johnny liked Howie and he didn't mind Gyda alone, without Spacely [*John Spacely, 80s East Village scenemaker*]. He liked Howie better than Gyda's boyfriends because they could talk about movies and music, and that left a little room for Gyda and I to be friends again without him going crazy. Other guys wanted to be friends with Johnny, too, but he didn't know how to make friends. He seemed to only be able to be friends with women—two at a time.

Anyway, John Lydon called us later that night—we had a phone by then—and he wanted to hang out with Johnny. I don't remember how he got our phone number, maybe I gave it to him, ha ha ha! Maybe Gyda did! Gyda wanted him to call because she wanted to get together with him, actually. She didn't have a boyfriend right then. Cheetah wasn't around, or she was between Cheetah and Spacely or something. So she wanted John Lydon to call and come over. And he did call. But Johnny told him, "Nah, we're not doing anything, we're just going to sleep!" Ha ha ha! He didn't want him coming over! And Gyda was like, *Oh, please!*

But he didn't want him there, because then Lydon would know where he lived and he didn't want anybody knowing where he lived. Of course, everybody knew!

So he turned Johnny Rotten down that night. I thought it would be interesting to have him over to our place. But of course—no. That would have been just too much fun for me and Gyda!

Yeah, that was a weird night. Then Johnny had a huge breakout of shingles on his legs because he was so stressed over Iggy!

He was in pain from that for most of his life. That was herpes and it was very painful. He would tell me he could barely walk sometimes because of this burning pain. He would have these lesions all over him, all over his back and legs, even his cock. His nerves were getting bad from working so hard and not getting enough rest. It must have been horrible. It definitely interfered with our sex life. I kept telling him to go get some Acyclovir or Zovirax, which cut the outbreaks down to like a day. I started taking it—you take it every day and it prevents them. He didn't have to be in that pain. But he chose not to go for treatment.

As far as I know, he had shingles all his life. He told me that his mother had genital herpes when she was pregnant or when she was giving birth, and that is a way you can get it—at birth, through your mother. It's possible. Or maybe he got it from some hooker, I don't know. I know he had it when I met him because I got it from him. But I only got it on my hand, on one finger, which is unusual, but you can get it anywhere. I must have touched his back during an outbreak, and I've had it there ever since. That's the only place I ever had it—just that one finger—but it was so painful. It's like this burning red line. Hopefully I never passed it on to anybody, I don't think I did. I would bandage myself up, and I only got it when I was very stressed out. He had it constantly because he was always stressed out. And he liked it like that—he enjoyed being angry, and if he wasn't angry, he'd try to find something that would *make* him angry.

⌘

I spent time with Anya Phillips that year, right before she died. I went
to see her and James Chance perform, I remember Lisa Robinson was
there. Anya had lost some hair but wore long falls and her own clothing
designs. She looked beautiful. Very thin.

She was doing a lot of painkillers, dilaudids, and heroin. She was
addicted to heroin and they were giving her dilaudid for the cancer so
she was really fucked up a lot of the time. But Johnny would let me go
out with her once in a while. I'd meet her usually at this place that served
chocolates and desserts, because she loved sweets, and she had lost a lot
of weight. She used to be sort of chubby. After she got cancer, she lost a
tremendous amount of weight but she just got more beautiful. She looked
really great right before she died. She looked really, really hot. Johnny
would never go with me. One time I asked him, "Why don't you come
with? You like Anya." He said, "No, I don't wanna see her like that."
But the way he acted, it seemed like he was afraid he was going to catch
something from her! He did not like being around people who were sick.

**Anya Phillips died of inoperable soft palate
cancer on June 19, 1981 in Valhalla, New York.**

Eileen Polk called me to tell me that Anya had died. I remember I
got off the phone and started crying. And I'll tell you what Johnny said—

he said, "Well, you knew it was gonna happen!" That's all he had to say. "You knew she was gonna die!" I was heartbroken. She was 26. I was 24.

A few days later James Chance called me and said they were having like a funeral "party" for her at a loft somewhere in Soho. Johnny wouldn't go, of course. Didn't want anything to do with the party people. But he said I could go, so I went with Eliot and Gyda.

I remember sitting in a corner of the room and watching what was going on, me and Gyda and Eliot and James. Lou Reed was there with Sylvia Morales and her fake tears. The whole thing seemed a little phony to me. People who didn't even know Anya as well as I knew her, crying over her and talking about her. I don't know. To me it was like, you got along, but I thought I knew her pretty well.

Eliot said he had some opium or something like that, something exotic, and James was all for that, so we left and went over to Eliot's and they were smoking whatever it was. I might have taken a puff or two, at that time I wasn't really doing any drugs. After a while me and James decided to go back downtown. We were in a taxi going down Third Avenue and we started screwing around with each other. When we got to 10th Street, there was Johnny standing at the corner. We were stopped at a red light, he saw me in the taxi with James and he ran up and threw the door open and pulled me out—told James he was gonna wrap that saxophone around his neck, ha ha ha!

James and I became pretty close after Anya's death. I remember dancing onstage when he played in Chicago one time, when I was living there in the mid-80s. I took the train up to Milwaukee and met him at his parents' place and spent a few days with him there, too. Johnny hated James, ha ha ha. James was very nice. So was his brother.

Yeah, Anya. Anya was too hip for words, you know. Too hip. She thought she was too hip. Little girl when I met her. Anya. Anya. Loved Anya. [3]

⌘

*He would go on these walks at night. I would
go over to visit and watch movies, and he
would go for a walk. And it'd be one hour, two
hours, three hours, four hours, and I'd be like,
Where is this guy? He went to the corner to
get a paper, what the fuck? "Oh yes, he's on
one of his walks." He's on a walk? You know.
She knew that something was up but she was
in major denial about it. So he just started,
like, leaving her.*   — Gyda Gash

I used to keep a diary back then and I wrote down what was going on
every day.  Even if I wrote just a sentence, I knew what had happened
that day and I could look it up. And it was at that time Johnny started
playing this disappearing act. He was disappearing for longer and longer
periods of time. He would get up in the morning, eat his breakfast and
come back, read the paper. And then he'd say, "I'm going out for a walk"
or whatever, I'm going to the store. And he would disappear for hours
and hours. I didn't know where he went—well, I had an idea. But I
would just wait for him. He was driving me crazy.

He kept complaining about my drinking, it was like a big concern
of his. He was the one who dragged me to my first AA meeting. I didn't
want to go! I think it was in Gramercy, because I remember I dragged
some other people there later on, ha ha ha! After a while I got into it and

started going every day. I tried to get Gyda to go with me, and another friend, Gail Merksamer, who was friends with Gyda, too. But Gail never got sober; she died a few years later.

Anyway, Johnny went with me that first time and he was very supportive. He had his arm around me, he was holding my hand, "Oh, come on." People kept coming up to me and trying to introduce themselves, you know how the people are in AA, very friendly. But I didn't want to talk to anybody. I was totally shy, I was humiliated and very hostile towards everyone. I didn't want to meet anyone, I didn't want to be there, didn't think I belonged there. I was only 24 years old and I was *not* an alcoholic!

He sat there next to me the whole meeting. They said, "Does anybody want to say anything?" and he grabbed my hand and tried to raise it, so I would say something—and I just wanted to hit him, ha ha ha! Afterwards we walked home and he was saying, "Oh, those people were nice," and I was pissed off because I wasn't ready for it and I didn't want somebody else to force me into doing that. It's a big step, you know? It's hard enough just going to AA, let alone having somebody drag you there when you don't want to go and you're not ready. He was telling me I was ready, I'm an alcoholic, and I didn't like it.

But I did it; I did it for him. I would get up in the morning, I'd go to my AA meeting, then I got a job, I would go to work, and I'd go to the New School a couple nights a week, I took a sewing class—I was signing up for all these classes, trying to keep busy. He started letting me stay home from concerts. He was so happy when he'd come home and find me alert and conscious and sitting up waiting for him in my slip. He would kiss me and say, "Why can't you be like this all the time?"

So I was trying to stay sober, and I kept telling him that my sobriety meant more to me than anything. I tried everything to stop drinking. I went for any kind of holistic healing, psychiatrists. I tried to heal myself. I got into all the crazy health stuff, vitamins, enemas in the morning,

Bach flower remedies, homeopathics, anything I thought would stop me from drinking, I became obsessed with it. Counting days and all this crap. Even witchcraft—I joined the church of Wicca. And I went for a lot of therapy, group and individual.

I even took Johnny to therapy with me once. It was this group of women, mainly, with their husbands. They were all alcoholics and they were having problems with their husbands and we would have a group session each week, so one week I made him come with me. We'd go around the room and everybody would talk about their problems, what's going on, opening up and talking to each other. When it was my turn I said, "Well, this is what's going on, he disappears and I've been trying to stay sober and I don't know what to do." Then we got to Johnny and they said, "Well, what *is* going on with you? Why don't you tell us?" He said, "Nothing. Nothing." You know? "Everything's fine."

Afterwards I was like, What—you know, why can't you open up and tell us? "I'm not gonna open up in front of those people! And I have nothing to tell." He was totally in denial. Like he was just *perfect*, and he didn't want anyone to hear any dirt on him. I could confront him with hard evidence that he was doing something behind my back and he'd still deny it to the death.

He swore that there was nothing going on. He just wanted to take long walks, you know, *every day*. I found a motel receipt once in his pocket and I confronted him about that. He said, "Oh, I've been going to this motel and I meet there with her, but you can go there—here, I'll give you the key. All I do is go there and read the paper in the morning." Then I got reports from other people that he's meeting Linda over at Anna Sui's. Walter Lure would say shit: "Oh yeah, he just goes over there and fucks her!" And I'm going *nuts* because he won't tell me the truth about anything! He's just going for a walk, you can imagine it. And I'm trying to stay sober all this time.

The whole thing was so shady and despicable now that I look back

on it. He was keeping up this front. I had no one to talk to because he
kept me separate, I wasn't friends with any of the other guys or women.
He kept me in the dark.

> *I knew from the get-go! I knew, I knew—*
> *That in the back of the fucking van, that*
> *fucking cunt was putting her toes under the*
> *seat, trying to tickle Johnny's ass. I'm like,*
> *'What the fuck is this girl doing, she's after*
> *your man! She is—You gotta watch her. You*
> *gotta watch her.' [Roxy] was in denial about*
> *it. She was actually thrilled that Johnny*
> *seemed happier, lighter, he was paying more*
> *attention to her, she even stopped drinking.*
> *It was a good time for them. But Linda's*
> *flirtatiousness and her perseverance, and*
> *his attraction to cruelty and insanity and*
> *domination, and this having two women thing,*
> *and the lying—that allure was too strong to*
> *maintain this healthy period that they had*
> *come upon. Because they were both in a very*
> *healthy period, very productive ... You know,*
> *it was brighter before the darkness. It was a*
> *good time, and it just fell apart after that.*
> *— Gyda Gash*

And there was another incident. One day Johnny went to one of
the stores where he used to buy his posters to see Caroline Munro, she

was there doing an in-store event. And I didn't want to go that day, so he was going to go by himself. Linda called me after he left and she says, "Where's Johnny, where's Johnny?"

I told her, "He went to see Caroline Munro, she's signing autographs down at Forbidden Planet" or wherever the hell it was. It was no big concern for me. But for her—"Oh, he's going to go see Caroline Munro, the movie actress?" She wanted to run down there and keep an eye on him! You know? I didn't feel like *I* had to keep an eye on him. But if he did leave me or cheat on me, I would have expected it would be with someone like Caroline Munro, not fuckin' Little Linda!

I was like, "Look: what do you care where my boyfriend is? Stop worrying about him so much. Start worrying about where *your* boyfriend is, OK?" And stop asking me where he is every two seconds, because that's what she was doing at that point. She was really getting on my nerves.

Well, a week or two later I got the mail one day, and there was this one envelope that felt like it had pictures inside, so I opened it up. Sure enough, here were these pictures of Linda and Johnny at this thing that I didn't go to! She showed up there and they took pictures of the two of them together. And I was just—*oooh!* So I called her up: "What are you doing? I'm coming over."

I went over to her place with the pictures and I walked in and I was like, fuming. She said, "What's the matter?" I said, "So, remember that day," and I ran it back to her and asked if she had gone there to meet Johnny. She denied knowing anything about it. I said, "Oh, really?" And I threw the pictures down, and I looked at her, and I just walked out.

After that she was calling me up and I said, "Look: you lied to me, and you know what? Now I don't want you talking to him at all." But it wasn't because I thought they were fucking. It was because she had lied to me. When I asked her did she go with him there, she flat-out lied to me. She betrayed me. She was trying to make me look like a fool and I wasn't going to have that.

She didn't care about Johnny at all. She didn't even like him. When I would ask her, "What's going on, why are you so worried about Johnny all the time," why are you doing these things, she'd say, "I don't want anything to do with your *boyfriend!*" You know? "I don't want your boyfriend!" She denied it every time.

All I knew was that she was stepping over the line. She had lied to me for some reason. But *he* totally denied it, too. "What are you, crazy? Nothing's going on, she's just my friend," and yeah, maybe that's all that they were at that point, who knows! I don't know. Maybe I pushed him into a deal with her. Who knows.

I guess I figured if he *was* doing that to me, if he was in fact having an affair, like he'd had with me, he would have hidden it a lot better than that! He wouldn't even talk to Rosana in front of me. When she was going to be around, I didn't go around. He would tell me if she planned on showing up at a show and I would stay away. I didn't want to see him with her, either. I never saw her, I never spoke to her till much later—he tried to keep us separate. He sent her away on vacations, he was trying to keep me a secret from his wife. He kept up appearances with his wife long after we got together. He didn't want her to know, but of course she must have! Same with Mitch's wife, Arlene—he kept it up with her, too, when he first started seeing me. Phoning her every day. Playing with everyone's emotions. But he was best friends with Linda, everybody knew it, they were always together!

And I wasn't going to the shows much anymore; by then, I didn't care. I was perfectly comfortable staying in the motel room and not having to go to the show. I'd stay in and read and have some time to myself. I mean, I still toured, I went with them, but I stayed more and more away from the shows, mainly because I didn't want to be around Linda anymore. I was sick of Linda.

And Linda, there was no way she could *not* go to a show. She had to be in the spotlight or whatever, where the excitement was. What "Little Linda" was all about was money and fame—any way she could get it. She went out with Joey until she realized that John was the one in charge and the one who would have money in the end, the way he squirreled it all away.

And Johnny loved the chase, and that someone liked him—no matter how ugly she was. He just wanted a friend and some excitement, and maybe to take something away from Joey. [4]

⌘

Then finally we had this big blow-up in Paris where I actually physically beat her up. Yeah. On the street in Paris.

I lost my mind because I'm not really a violent person—I mean, I don't usually go and attack somebody unless they're paying for it, ha ha ha! I'm not the kind of person who's like, "I'm gonna kick your ass" and go out and fight somebody.

I just saw red that night. I spotted Johnny and Linda walking together after I told them to stay away from each other, and I went tearing out of the Alexandra Hotel and came running up behind her and literally threw her to the ground. I don't even remember what happened, but Johnny was pulling me off of her, and the French cops came running, wearing the funny hats and capes, wanting to arrest us—and I was still kickin' her! I heard she was limping around for the rest of the tour. Nobody knew what had happened, Johnny wasn't going to say anything and I guess she didn't say anything, either.

I left the next day. I drank everything that was in the refrigerator,

and I made him give me every cent he had, and he gave me every cent
and told me I should go home. How sorry he was.

I was very upset. I was also angry that poor Joey didn't see. He was
blind to it all. Joey was like, "Where did Cynthia go?" and he had no
clue what had happened. Other times I'd be so pissed off at Johnny that
I wouldn't even talk to Linda and Joey, and Joey would be going, "Well,
what's the matter with her, what's the matter?" He had no clue what
was going on, you know? And I didn't, either—well, I knew Johnny was
pissin' me off! *She* was pissin' me off! But it's like Joey didn't even see!

I never thought my suspicions could really be true until Paris. Even
then I didn't know what to think. John was home every day, even though
his walks at night got longer. I also didn't question Joey, although he had
been asking Linda what I was upset about. I no longer wanted to talk to
her, nor did I want her talking to my boyfriend. I hated her, and I was
pissed that he would disobey me and go walking down the street with her
like that. Fuck that bitch! She's the only one who's *ever* taken me there.
All my friends hated him and wanted me to leave him anyhow, but I
wouldn't, and where would I go?

Oh yeah, it got worse, it got so much worse. People would come up
to me and they were like, *I'm so sorry*—they were feeling sorry for me
and shit, and I didn't want that.

It seemed that everyone was talking and making fun of them but me
and Joey. We didn't see it because it didn't go on in front of us. She was
still with him and I was, of course, with John. But they all knew, except
me and Joey. It was that blatant. Johnny couldn't or wouldn't stop. It
was like an obsession. Hiding Linda and running around, all that shit.
Everybody should have just sat down and straightened it out. Joey should
have said something. *Immediately*. And I should have, too. Instead of just
running away, I should have stayed there, I should have put it out in the
open and confronted it.

But I didn't. I took all his money and flew to London, then home by myself, drunk all the way, and stayed drunk in New York with my friends Roger Mayer and Connie—a different Connie. Roger was a British guitar effects genius who I had met through some other musicians. He remained a very close friend through Marc and Johnny. I'd go to his place for R & R. He made Jimi Hendrix effects boxes. Johnny didn't like them.

After Paris, that was it—I was like, No more, no more of this. And I told Johnny, "You know what? You're not going to talk to her anymore. I don't want her around, I don't like her, and I don't want you talking to her or having anything to do with her anymore." So whenever he saw her, he tried to give this smile or whatever—it just got really tense. Everything got tense. And Joey would come over to me and he's like, "What happened?" You know, "What is going on, what happened?" And I'd just say, "Ask her."

I know some people claim that Joey and Linda broke up mid-1981, but they didn't. She was still with him on that tour. I remember Johnny telling me at some point, Oh, she wants to leave Joey but she has nowhere to go. She doesn't have any money to get an apartment. She's going to work for Anna Sui or something. She did live with Anna Sui for a while when she first left Joey.

I don't know exactly when we were in Paris that year, but I remember that day was sort of cold. And I remember listening to the Psychedelic Furs, their second album—I was feeling depressed, I know that's what I was listening to.

*Talk Talk Talk* **was released June 1981; the Paris incident probably took place on or about November 17, 1981.**

*She did it out of respect for their relationship,
and caring. You know, the black clothes went,
the S&M gear went—out came the white frills,
the pinafores, the hair, everything got lighter,
the makeup got lighter...she was staying
sober for him. He would monitor her, her
food, what did she eat and all this, and she
wouldn't drink, she wouldn't drink, and it was
working, it was working. His domination and
control, for some reason, the co-dependence
of that, she was able to get sober for a time.
And it was really wild to see. I remember
going to Umberto's with them once and being
so happy that she wasn't drinking, it was like,
Wow! I was excited for her, because it seemed
like this could be the start of something
great. I mean, she was a completely different
person. Prior to that, she was drunk all
the time. I mean, all the time. And then he
started fucking around with this fucking cunt.
At that time, you know? So it shattered her, I
think. When she had tried so much. I think it
blew her mind.   — Gyda Gash*

⌘

We hated the holidays because they were very lonely and there was
nothing to do. We really didn't have any family in New York. He was
depressed around the holidays, especially after his father died. And he

always got fat. Christmas was always sad for John. He missed being a kid, and his dad.

That year at Christmas I got myself a job working at Macy's. I had been going to AA, dragging Gyda and Gail there. I just wanted to keep myself busy and show him that I wasn't helpless and hopeless or whatever. I did everything he wanted me to do, and I bought lots of Christmas gifts that year. All the money that I made, I bought gifts for him and for the apartment.

One day he came to see me at Macy's and I was really happy, I was telling him all about the presents and what we were going to do for Christmas. All of a sudden he started crying. I asked him what's wrong and he said he had to go to Florida. And I said, "I thought we were going to spend Christmas here together!" He just kept saying, "I have to go, I have to go, you were doing so good, you're doing so good." I told him not to go but he just kept saying, "I have to, I have to." So I said, "Well, okay, can I go with you?" He said, "No, I gotta go by myself," and that I should go see my mother. He was really, really distraught over something, and then I started getting upset. Finally I just said, "Well, go ahead," you know. Whatever you do, it's not gonna affect my sobriety, I want that more than anything else. And he just left me there in Macy's.

I don't know what was going on, but it had something to do with Linda. Maybe she wanted to go to Florida with him, or wanted him to spend Christmas with her. I didn't speak to her anymore by then. She must have been driving him nuts, and he was feeling sad and guilty. It was a lot of stress for him to lead this double life.

I still gave him all these things he wanted, that I'd bought for him for Christmas. There were lots of little presents, like old books, some biographies that he'd been looking for, I went to the bookstores and found them. And I remember he cried then, too. He said it was the best Christmas he'd ever had since he was a kid. He was so happy.

But he went to Florida without me that year.

# 1982

*If there was a big party or a big event, they wouldn't go as a couple. It wasn't that kind of a thing. He wasn't into it—he hated everything, he hated everybody.* — Gyda Gash

*I dunno if we had fun together...Most of the time, at least a couple of us were not talking. In 1982, no one talked to each other. We still played shows, so it was hard, but there were good times too.* — Johnny Ramone

SO WHEN *DID* JOEY AND LINDA break up? It was weird, because I really didn't hear anything about it. I remember wondering or asking, "What about the bitch?" or something, and he said, "Oh, she doesn't live there anymore. She moved. They broke up." Like that. I didn't know she broke up with him! Nobody knew when they broke up, nothing was ever said about it.

"Linda, where's Linda?" Nobody knew. She was gone. I didn't know where she was. She had left Joey and gotten her own apartment. Well, how the hell did she afford to get her own apartment? Who knows, maybe Johnny paid for it. She was living over on 23rd Street, I found out after a while—and I guess he moved in there eventually.

When she first left, she moved in with Anna Sui. Walter Lure lived there too, and he told Gyda he would see Johnny over there.

Johnny stopped going out around that time. He'd walk with me to the Ritz to get me and my friends in, then he would leave. I was sober most of the time, so he started letting me go out with Gyda and Howie Pyro. I don't know why he didn't want to go out anymore.

After Linda, Joey had a girlfriend named Angela [*Galletto*] for a little while, who he met here in California. She and her sister Camille both moved to New York. Camille started going out with Monte and moved in with him, and Angela lived with Joey in his apartment on Ninth Street. I don't know what happened to those sisters, but Johnny didn't like them.

I remember when MTV first started, the Ramones got tickets to the MTV New Year Eve's Party, the first one [*December 31, 1982*]. Johnny didn't want to go but I went. Bow Wow Wow played, and Duran Duran. Joey was there with Angela, or maybe Holly from Holly and The Italians. Mitch and Arlene were there, I sat with them. I think Dee Dee and Vera were there, too. Linda wasn't there. It was fun.

# 1983

ONE NIGHT JOHNNY SAID he was going to go for a walk and get a slice of pizza. It took ten hours. He disappeared, and this time he was gone all night. He'd never been gone all night before.

We were supposed to go on tour in a couple of days [*the US/Canada tour that began April 8, 1983, and ended June 30*] and he had told me to be ready to go on a certain day. So I was packing everything up to go. When he finally came home in the morning he told me not to bother packing since I wasn't going. *What?* What do you mean I'm not going? He said, "No, you're staying here, I don't want you going with." And I just threw a fit. We had a big fight, and he took his stuff and left. He went out on tour and I was left at home.

That's when I said, *Fuck this, fuck everything,* and gave up on trying to stay sober for him. I had a bottle of nembutols or some sort of downer—librium, that's what it was. He had sent me to see a shrink and they put me on librium, because I would get extremely nervous at night when, two o'clock in the morning, he wasn't home yet and I would just be waiting for him. I had been trying to stay away from drinking but it was on and off, and all my friends kept saying, "Forget about him and come out." I'd go to AA and stop for a while, then I'd go on a binge, but I hadn't been out in a long time.

Well, when he left and went on tour without me, that was it. I took the librium and that's when I started drinking and going out again. I started going to The Park Inn and all those bars on Avenue A, the Aztec and A7, with people like Ty Stix, and got into the hardcore and skinhead scene. Or I'd run over to Revenge at Third and St. Mark's and hang out. The first time, I went out in some Betsey Johnson shit and I felt sort of out of place—too sissy. So I changed my look a little, got some combat boots and started dressing a little more punk rock, hardcore. It was like a throwback! It was funny, because it hadn't been that long in between, but all of a sudden everybody was very "punk" again, with mohawks and fins and dyed hair and combat boots instead of the New Romantic stuff. So I started dressing like that and hanging out.

> *Some people were a bit concerned about Roxy, because she would get drunk when Johnny wasn't there (or on tour) and if he heard about it he would get mad. People went out of their way to protect her and her reputation because she was well liked.*
> — *Eileen Polk*

This is when I met Johnny Angel, from the band Thrills from Boston. I met him at the Park Inn. He got pretty obsessed with me, he wanted me to marry him! Everybody wanted me to leave Johnny for him, ha ha ha. He was always jealous of Johnny.

> *I had seen her many times with JR, with whom I was acquainted, as Thrills were the Ramones' perennial opening act in Boston. But we didn't speak. I met her for real through*

*Ty Stix, former Heartbreakers and Senders drummer, spring 1983. JR was on tour, she was at Park Inn on Avenue A with Stix. I was living on Avenue B at the time, unemployed and out of bands. She liked my porkpie hat, apparently. She invited me back to her place, whose address I recognized as the place Thrills stored their gear when we played NYC. We watched horror films, Ty conked out, Cynthia and I had sex on her stove and that began the relationship. We weren't really an item beyond the sort of private thing we had. She saw herself as JR's girlfriend, even though he was already with Linda. When the Ramones were due to return from the 1983 US tour [end of June], I realized that I had no interest in keeping the furtiveness going and I hated NYC at that point. So, I returned to Boston to play music again and she did what she did, which was drink and pick up guys.*
*— Johnny Angel [1]*

One night in August, my friend Ty Stix called me up. He was the drummer for Johnny Thunders. He was like a big clown, but he was nice so I hung out with him once in a while. Anyway, he came over and said, "You gotta get out of the house, come on, I'm going to a bar."

So we went to The Park Inn and I was drinking and I met this guy Seth Macklin. He said he was in some punk rock band, a stupid name [*Sub-Zero Construction*]. He was nobody, you know? But we got talking.

Johnny was coming back from somewhere he went to play that

night and I knew that I had to be home at a certain hour. So this guy said, "Well, let me walk you home," and I said OK. So he walked me down the street and he wanted to come up or something and I said, "No you can't, I live with my boyfriend." I don't think I told him who I lived with or anything.

We were sitting across the street from 85 East 10th, on the steps of the building across the street, talking, and time passed. I told him my boyfriend would be back and I had to go upstairs. He started kissing me. Right then the van pulled up and Johnny got out. And I said, "Oh, shit," you know? Ha ha ha. Johnny saw me sitting there and he came walking over and said to me, "Get upstairs." I didn't say anything, I just got up.

And this guy, I don't know what he thought—I guess he didn't know what was going on, he just saw this guy walking at us, looking sorta mad. The next thing I knew, he punched Johnny or something, knocked him down. He was a little guy and Johnny was supposed to be so tough. But Johnny wasn't looking and he sucker-punched him. Once he was down, the guy was really quite fast, it was just like *boom—boom—boom*. He started kicking Johnny while he was down, in the head. And he had like steel-toed boots, and he kept on kicking him and then the blood started spurting out. I'm screaming for help and trying to make him stop. He finally did and he ran off. I was all bloody and so was Johnny. I was wearing this pink jacket and I got down and I was trying to hold on to him. Some people stopped and I said, "Will somebody call an ambulance?" I stayed with him and the ambulance came and they took him away.

The Ramones had played a show in Queens on Saturday night, August 13. The attack occurred in the early morning hours of Sunday, August

14, 1983 (3:50 a.m., according to *The New York Times*). Johnny's skull was fractured; he was taken to St. Vincent's Hospital in Manhattan, where he underwent four hours of surgery. The band did not perform again until December 20.

He was pretty much unconscious when the ambulance came. That guy must have kicked him, like—I don't know, he did something. John had some sort of brain damage, he had to have surgery. And I had to go to the police station to give some sort of statement.

Then some reporters came to the apartment—I don't know how they found out, but my girlfriend Elida was there and I guess she let them in, she had a big mouth and started saying a bunch of crap. The reporters took pictures of some pictures of me and Johnny that were on the wall. The next day, it was on the front page of the *New York Post*: "Rocker stomped!" It was just stupid.

**Rocker Fights For Life - Superstar stomped in 10th St. rage over woman he loves**
— *Front page*, New York Post, *August 15, 1983*

This went on for, like, all week, front page news. There were pictures, all this crap written—"stomped in feud over this woman!" They had pictures of me sitting at the police station with a beer, all this stuff. Crazy.

### Jealous Rage

NEW YORK (AP) – The street fight that landed punk rocker Johnny Ramone in the hospital with a skull fracture apparently began because his view of his relationship with a female friend "was different than (what) she thought," a detective said.

Police say the fight broke out early Sunday when Ramone, 29, who founded the punk rock group The Ramones, went into "a fit of jealous rage" when he saw 27-year-old Cynthia Whitney outside her apartment with another man.

"She thought it was an open relationship, and she was free to be with other people," said Detective Dennis Carroll. "He assumed his relationship with the girl was different than she thought."

Seth Macklin, 22, a member of the band Sub-Zero Construction, was charged with first-degree assault in the case.

In a statement to police, Macklin said Ramone "started the fight by hitting me with a shoulder bag, and I hit him back. I defended myself and hit him two or three times. He fell and hit his head on the car door and sidewalk."

*– Associated Press*

I didn't go to the hospital with him. I didn't go at all; I was told *she* was there. Bunch of people kept coming over, friends of mine, old girlfriends, they were bringing alcohol and getting drunk and partying it up in the apartment with me.

*I got the call the next day, she told me in a drunken haze, "Oh this happened, and the [reporters] are coming to the door," and I'm like, Reporters? Kicked in the head, head injury? So I ran over to the apartment, thinking, Oh, my best friend, oh my God, this is terrible— and here I am, you know, to console my best friend. She's sitting there with a can of beer, sprawled out on the bed. She's got like some fuckin diddleybop from Boston, "Ooh Roxy, what can I do for you?" And another one, they're coming out of the woodwork. I'm like, "You don't need me!" And then she's telling the story over again, and she's got the Post, with her picture in it—She loved it so much! I'm like, "What about Johnny, is he gonna be OK?" And she's like, "Ohhh, he might be brain-damaged! Ha ha ha ha ha!" It was like, Woooooo! Crazy. It was crazy. ... I remember the reporters came to the house, and she had this old friend, another fuckin tragic case, her friend Elida Ramirez, another girl we used to dance with. And Elida told—ha ha!—told the reporters that she was from the cotton-gin Whitneys or something, so there was this big article—"Heiress Cynthia Whitney," and she was like, "Look what it says! Ha ha ha!" And I'm like, What about the guy in*

*the hospital, you know? Anyway, it was like a*
*riot. A riot. She loved it.  — Gyda Gash*

Then his mother flew into town and my mother flew in, and his
mother was trying to pack up all his stuff and my mother was trying to
pack up all my stuff. I was drunk with my friends and the two of them
just started packing everything away. They decided to put everything in
storage. At that point old Stella was really a nagging bitch, whereas my
mother was a saint and didn't say much to her. She just flew in because
she wanted Stella to see that I had a mother—a real lady. And rich.

I don't know what the hell they were doing, I was so drunk—I kept
trying to get to the hospital to see him but I didn't go, because I didn't want
to go like that. And his mother was screaming at me, "You just better stay
away from him!" And anyhow, I guess Linda was there!

The next thing I knew, everything in our apartment was packed up
and they're moving everything out. All of a sudden everything's gone,
even my clothes. I didn't even realize.

Finally, about a week later, they let Johnny out of the hospital. He
came home and everything in our apartment had been cleared out and I
was leaving. I told him I was going back to Chicago just to get away from
this nightmare for a while. They had shaved his head and it was bandaged.
And he wasn't yelling—he was different. He was very nice. It was like
he'd had a lobotomy or something. I remember getting in the taxi and he
told me he loved me and he would call me. I was only going to be gone for
a week or so. I remember him standing there, waving that little wave that
he does, and crying, and we drove away and I went to Chicago.

There were too many things decided for us, what we were going
to do. His mother showed up, my mother showed up—all of a sudden
they're taking everything out of the apartment and I don't know what

the hell's going on. I didn't even take anything with me to Chicago! Everything was left in New York. I went with *nothing*, not even any clothes. I just got on the plane and left with my mother, because my mother didn't think I should be there. Especially the way his mother was acting: "Oh, your daughter better leave New York!" As if it was all my fault, what happened.

He didn't seem to blame me at the time. Afterwards he did, after everybody told him to blame me. But it wasn't my fault. It was mostly his fault for not coming home.

There were a lot of rumors about what happened that night. One rumor was that Johnny Angel was the one who attacked Johnny Ramone. That didn't make any sense because Johnny Angel had already moved back to Boston by then, and that's where he was that night. We were still seeing each other, I'd go up there weekends and he called me all the time. But he had nothing to do with this [2].

There was also a rumor that Seth Macklin and I had made some sort of deal to beat up Johnny Ramone. Well, there was no conspiracy; I was not involved with Macklin at all. But some time later, Johnny told me that he was approached by someone close to the Ramones who wanted to know if he wanted Macklin whacked for like $2000. Johnny said no, which I thought was very forgiving of him, or else he was just too damn miserly.

Actually, none of my friends seemed very upset about what had happened to Johnny. It seemed like they all thought that's what he deserved because he'd been so mean, such an asshole to everybody and to me. People would say, "How could you be with him? I hate him." You know? That's what everybody used to tell me: "I *hate* him, you gotta leave him. *I hate him.*"

But the reason I left wasn't about the relationship. It was because I was on the front page of the newspaper and people were in and out of the apartment, his mother was screaming at me, and everything that was going on at the hospital, *Linda* was over there… My mother was just trying to protect me. She thought I should get out of there for a little while. She saw the condition I was in and what a mess everything was. All the stress I had been under. I needed a break.

I had been trying for so long to be what he wanted me to be—sober. And most of the time, I *was* sober. I never drank around him after we were together. I don't know why the only thing anybody has to say about me is that I was an alcoholic. I would get drunk every once in a while, I mean, maybe four times a year! When he would go out of town or something, I would call some friends or they'd come over and, "Oh, what are you doing, well, let's go out to a bar!" Everybody would want me to party with them!

Going and staying at my mother's made thing easier for me. It was simple. But it wasn't like I was "leaving him"—I did intend to come back to New York.

I guess I was sick of the way things had been going. He had wanted me to get sober and be a certain way for so long, and then when I did it, he didn't want that either. Looking back on it now, I think he made such a big deal about my drinking as a way of distracting me from what *he* was doing with Linda.

Johnny was always private, he always wanted to keep me and our personal life insulated, but over time I had gotten more and more cut off. I went along with it all for a long time, but you have to remember how young I was. Even though I'd packed a lot into those few teenage years before we got together, I really wasn't done yet. I didn't have a mind or personality of my own anymore apart from being with Johnny Ramone. I was like a fixture.

But I did not think I was leaving him. We both seemed a lot happier with each other by having a little distance right then, but we had no intention of breaking up. I only meant to be in Chicago for a little while. Then all this other stuff happened.

# 1984–89

DURING THE BREAK-UP, all of a sudden here was his chance to see what it would be like to be with "Little Linda" all the time. And he hated it. As soon as he could, he was on the telephone, calling me, calling me, calling me. He called me constantly. Johnny spoke to me every single day, and always told me how much he hated Linda. When I was away from him, he said he needed to speak to me on the phone or he'd go crazy. He needed me to tell him what he should be doing. Believe it or not. He really had no friends.

I got to Chicago and I was really depressed. I didn't have any clothes or anything—well, my mother went out and bought me whatever I needed. I was just going to stay in Chicago for a little while and then go back home. But I ended up staying for five years.

His mother came and my mother came and they cleared all our stuff out, but he didn't give up that apartment. He kept that apartment for another seven years. That was our apartment, and he kept it so that he could leave *her* apartment every day, and go back home, and sit on the telephone with me. And he had some gadget, too, where he could make long-distance phone calls from pay phones and he didn't have to put any money in. So he could stop anywhere—he walked a lot—he'd walk around with a little transistor radio to his ear, listening to the ball game, and he'd have to call me up to tell me something or ask me something. So he'd just stop in a phone booth and call me. I was in Chicago, but it was like we weren't even away from each other.

I don't know where he got that thing. He bought it from

somewhere—very illegal! Must have ripped off the phone companies for a lot of money over the years.

When he couldn't talk to me, he bombarded me with postcards and letters with stick figures of me and him. All those letters that I had from him, he barely said a word. It was mainly pictures or else he drew stick figures. One postcard I remember had a stick figure with a sad face and the words "I miss you," and two stick figures with one grabbing the other's tits. He was a "sad dog," he'd say, when I wasn't there.

We talked all the time about when was I coming home. I said I was coming back, I was supposed to come back right away, but I just stayed and stayed on in Chicago. I wanted to stay there. Basically for years I had been alone, I didn't have any friends, I wasn't *allowed* to have any friends, I wasn't *allowed* to talk to anybody. That's how I had to live. And I did, for him. For Johnny.

But in Chicago I had a ton of friends. And I was having such a good time, I didn't want to go back to New York and his crap and that fucking Linda and everything else. I couldn't bear even to think about it. I wanted to stay in Chicago. Finally I told him I wanted to go back to school. And I was still young enough where it wasn't that far out of—it wasn't that far out, ha ha ha! I just felt that I was wasting my time, being in the background and doing nothing with my life.

Well, he said, find an apartment and he would pay the rent. At that point, my mother had paid our rent for years. For seven years, she paid the rent every month. I mean, this guy didn't have to pay for *anything*, you know? He never had to pay rent. *He never even had to pay rent.*

He got me my own apartment. He was paying for it. He paid for everything. I mean, here he is paying for me to live there and basically whatever I wanted. So yeah, I was having a good time! [1]

And yet the whole time I was living in Chicago, Johnny kept our 10th Street apartment. Whether he was sleeping there at night or what he was doing during the day, I couldn't say. I can only tell you what I know, which is that he called me every day, all day long, and he was calling from that apartment and he was paying for that apartment. *And* paying for my apartment in Chicago.

Was he was doing all that because he wanted me to stay in Chicago? No, I was the one who decided to stay in Chicago. Maybe he wanted to keep it the way it was. Maybe *I* wanted to keep it the way it was, too. But we still planned on getting back together.

⌘

I had been in Chicago for seven or eight months when I got a phone call one day from Johnny Angel, who told me that my friend Gail Merksamer had died. Gail died up in Boston with Johnny Angel's band—everybody was related, you know? She met Johnny Angel through me and started hanging out with a guy in his band. She went up to Boston to see them play, I guess she'd been sober a little bit, and she did heroin there and she died [2]. She came from Scarsdale and her family was rich, real rich. She was tragic, too.

I was really upset and I was making arrangements to fly back to New York for Gail's funeral when Johnny called. He said, "What's the matter?" I told him Gail died. "What? What are you talking about? How did Carolyn die?" Meaning Carolyn my sister. I said, I didn't say Carolyn, I said Gail. "Oh, I thought you said Carolyn!"

Well, the next day I was getting ready to leave and I got a phone call from my sister's boyfriend. He was like all crazy and says, "You gotta help me, I can't wake up Carolyn." And I said, look, throw her in the shower, walk her around. And he said, "No, she won't move at all. You gotta come down here."

So I got in a taxi and I went down to where her boyfriend lived. And I went in and she was dead. She was in bed naked, had candles lit—she was beautiful. But she was dead. So I ran around the house and picked everything up, like needles and stuff, I wanted to hide all that before the paramedics got there. Then my mother arrived and my brother arrived and I left and went to a bar.

So that happened. That was 1984. I had to arrange everything for her funeral, everybody was too upset to do anything. Carolyn's funeral was beautiful. Men came from all over the country for it. She was very beautiful and sexy, she'd just turned 22. She could have gone to L.A. or New York to be an actress or model but she wanted to stay near my mom in Chicago, I guess.

It was just strange how Johnny called and said, "What do you mean, Carolyn's dead?" And then the next day she's dead.

He didn't come out for her funeral. I asked him to. But he didn't. He didn't handle death well. He'd never had to deal with any deaths except his father's.

After my sister died, my mother got very depressed and I didn't want to leave her alone. A few years later she jumped off a balcony—she tried to commit suicide and she almost did, but she survived the attempt.

⌘

I went back to New York to visit a few times. I remember I flew back in 1985 and Johnny took me and my friend Polly Gibson out shopping—

bought us furs at Aardvark. For some reason he was carrying some autographed baseballs in a paper bag and he set them down in the store. All of a sudden, he starts yelling, "Where's my balls? Where's my balls??!" and everybody busted out laughing!

He sent me an engagement ring around this time, too. It was gold with a quarter-carat round diamond. I don't like diamonds but I had wanted one from him because Vera and Linda used to flaunt theirs from Dee Dee and Joey. My best friend in Chicago, Regan Comstock [*transsexual model photographed by Francesco Scavullo*], told me it looked like a confirmation ring and to send it back. I did, and he sent me a bigger one, with the receipt! $500! I lost his ring in '94 in Cook County Jail, I never got another from him.

Whatever I asked him for, he got me, especially after I stopped drinking again in Chicago. I was sober for five years, from 1987–'91. I just quit drinking one day, I called him up and I said, "I quit," you know? He was so happy. And after five days of being quit, he bought me a camera—a video camera. Whatever I wanted, he would just buy it and send it to me. He bought me eight cats to start a cattery, he thought that would be a good hobby for me. Persians, flame-point Siamese, and Himalayan. All show cats, beautiful, expensive, and Johnny paid for every one of them. He would have supported any business I wanted to go into if I had just stayed sober.

I know he has a reputation for being cheap. But he was not cheap. At home he wasn't like that at all. He was very generous. He just didn't like owing anything so he paid in full in cash. He wasn't selfish and usually he wouldn't lie, except for his affairs. He always had to lead that double life. Little game, little fetish or whatever.

But he couldn't bring Linda anywhere—could not be seen with her! She couldn't be around any of the shows or anything anymore, after what she did to Joey. It must have been sort of a drag for *her* that she couldn't be around anybody else.

He kept the place on 10th Street, Linda didn't know about it, she
didn't know that he went there *every day* and hung out in the apartment
and called me from that phone. She didn't know about the little device
he carried around so that he could call me at every phone booth on every
block. Legs McNeil knew that! He said he'd see him around town,
jumping into the phone booth with this little device that paid for the
phone call. And calling me, calling me, all day [3]. I was thankful for
his daily morning calls. Knowing that he would be calling probably kept
me somewhat focused and coherent during some of those years when
I was otherwise incapacitated. And if it wasn't me, he would speak to
whoever was there and make sure I was still alive and OK. It seemed
like he loved me more when I was away from him. He always needed a
secret relationship. Something on the side. All of a sudden I was the on-
the-side, and it was a little exciting for him. I became the Other Woman
again—as I was in the beginning.

⌘

In Chicago everyone knew everyone, like CBGB days, and I was having
a ball. I went out every night. I had all the young boys hanging around
me, vying for my attention, and I was loving it! We went out in groups
there, my gang, me and all these boys—gay and straight. My best friends
were gay and I've always loved that lifestyle. I hung with transsexuals,
too, like Regan Comstock. I had all my gay boys, I participated in all the
gay activities, I lived in "Boy's Town." My aggressions and dominant
side finally came out around that time. I started changing—exploring
other, taboo or kinky sides of sex, getting more and more bizarre. I got

my first strap-on. I dressed like a gay leather daddy and had the best clothes. That's when people started the rumor that I'd had a sex change. The story was that Johnny Ramone paid for it, ha!

Yeah, I was doing things in Chicago. I was sober, I had a car and a condo and a 20-year-old boyfriend and I was loving life. Johnny and I were still talking every day. And he was sending me all this stuff all the time—whatever was in the house, whatever he collected—movies, tour posters, stuff, he'd send it all to me. Box it up and send it to me. At one point he started collecting art and sent me three Peter Max paintings of the Statue of Liberty. He was even packaging up groceries! He would go to the supermarket and buy all this food and send boxes constantly to me. Sending me food, sending me boxes of all his stuff, stuff we had at the apartment. And money—he'd send me, like, hundred dollar bills. There would be nothing in the letters, just pieces of paper folded over. Then people started breaking into my mailbox and taking them. He's sending me money every day, I'm getting money in the mail, I'm getting boxes of food, and he's paying my rent in Chicago. And I'm living with this other guy and hanging out with all these fags and transsexuals.

There was also a joke that went around New York for a while, or so I heard, that Linda had a boob job but Johnny was so cheap, he only paid for one boob. But actually, that was me. I never told anybody this, and I don't think Johnny did either, but that's exactly right—he paid for one of my boobs! But *not* because he was cheap.

It was 1989 or '90, right before I left Chicago for L.A. I had lost a lot of weight because without those empty beer calories, no weight would stay on me. I lost, like, twenty pounds or something, which is a lot for me, and I got really thin. And my breasts just deflated. They were big before and Johnny loved big breasts, you had to have big breasts or he didn't like you. Really—Rosana knows that, too, she says the same things that I do. I disliked Rosana at first, but later I realized there was no reason to, you know?

Anyhow, so I was deflating and I told Johnny, "I don't know what's going on, but I've gotta have a breast job immediately. I'm gonna go and get my breasts done, like—*this week!*" Ha ha ha! I had to! I mean, I couldn't move to California looking like that. Somehow I had gotten ten or twenty thousand dollars from somebody, so I was going to pay for it myself. And he goes, "Oh no no no, I don't want you spending any of your money, I'll pay for it." That's what he would always say when I said I wanted to buy this or that. And I was very careful with my money. I'll go out and look for a bargain, I won't just throw money around. I guess I should have taken that money and bought a fuckin' house! Back then I didn't think I needed to.

Anyhow, I said no, that I would pay for them and he said, "No, I'll pay for them." Finally we decided, you pay for half and I will pay for half. So yeah, he paid for one! And I paid for one.

And then I got addicted. I wasn't doing drugs or drinking, so I got addicted to cosmetic surgery. When I got out here, I just couldn't wait to go back and do something else. I looked so good when I moved out here, and then I just kept going back for more. I was only 35 years old, but I thought that's when I looked the best.

⌘

Whenever Johnny was in Chicago, I was with him. Like that tour when they played with Debbie Harry in Milwaukee—it was Debbie Harry's birthday—I was there with him. [*Escape From New York, with the Ramones, Debbie Harry, and the Tom Tom Club; Milwaukee was July 1, 1990, Harry's birthday.*] I went to that show with my boyfriend Tom—

Tomahawk. Me, Tom, and my friend Jane and her son drove up to see them. Tom got jealous and drunk and when Johnny and I were kissing goodbye, he threw a beer bottle at Johnny. Rude, nasty skinhead, thought he knew it all.

And Johnny flew out for my birthday one year, to take me to wrestling matches, WWF Wrestling. Yeah. He was very happy when I started watching wrestling!

By then it wasn't a sexual relationship. But there was never that much of a sexual relationship to begin with. I don't think he needed that much of a sexual relationship. He was looking more for companionship.

⌘

In the summer of 1989 I went to New York with some friends. I stayed with my friend Christos Skleros, who I met in Chicago, and Johnny came to see me and everything was pretty cool [4]. I had just gotten back to Chicago when my brother called and said, "Can you get over to such and such a hospital, 'cause mom is dead." Just like that. And I'm like, "*What?!*" "Yeah. Mom is dead. I'll meet you there."

I freaked out. I wanted to call Johnny, but of course I couldn't, because at that point he's not answering the phone. Finally my brother Kent reached him and told him I needed him and he flew to Chicago.

As it turned out, my mother wasn't dead. She had jumped from her balcony and survived, but she was in a coma for the next six months. She had never gotten over my sister's death. After she recovered enough, I decided to move to California, because that's where Johnny said he wanted to move. He said we were going to live together in California.

I was being so naïve back then. But it seemed ridiculous to me that he would want to be with Linda. She couldn't even show her face with him. Nobody had ever dumped me, and John told me every day that he loved me. And he still would not admit *anything* was going on between him and Linda. He wasn't married to her yet, and he refused to say that he was living with her. He told me he hated Linda, "I can't stand her," blah blah blah, and we're gonna get together again and everything's gonna be great, we're gonna move to California and all this. This is what he was telling me every day.

# 1990–98

MY BROTHERS HAD TAKEN control of some land after my mother's suicide attempt and in 1990 they gave it to me, to appease me and make me happy so that I would take care of her: "Give her all this stuff." Johnny couldn't stand it when I got this inheritance because he thought, "You're gonna leave me. You won't want me anymore. You don't need me now!" I would think that he'd be happy! But that didn't make him happy either. *Nothing* I did made him happy.

So I had all this land, it was mostly in Mississippi and it was such a mess, nobody even wanted to take care of it. They just didn't want to bother with it, so they gave it to me. It was like, I don't know, 1800 different lots—all these plots of land in Mississippi! There was so much money they didn't care about stuff like that, my family. They didn't. They had enough money that they didn't even have to bother with it.

So I sorted through all these papers, I went through every one of them and started sending bills to everybody, piecing them all together and trying to collect money from them. Then I tried to sell it all off because of the taxes and everything.

I got that inheritance in 1990 and that's when I moved to California, with my mother and my boyfriend Tomahawk. Tomahawk was a crossdresser, 12 years younger than me. His outward appearance was that of a tough Nazi skinhead punk street kid. He was very good-looking, he had this mile-high blue fin before he became skin, and a lot of tattoos— he looked like Woody Harrelson in *Natural Born Killers*. I disliked him when I first met him, but then we became close hanging out. He had a very bad temper, flew into jealous rages and was always ready to fight.

When I first got to L.A., I was doing a lot of extra work in movies and got myself and Tomahawk into SAG [*Screen Actors Guild, the movie actors' union*]. Tom was doing commercials, stunt and extra work, but he hated California. I got a couple of little parts and even did some casting, which I loved. My brothers wanted me to open a talent agency and tried to help me with that. I had a whole troupe of "alternative" types that depended on me for work. I was up early every day, calling in. I was sober.

And my relationship with Johnny was still the same—it was always the same! *It never changed.* He was still calling me every single day. Every single day. He would get really worried if he couldn't get in touch with me and he'd freak out if he couldn't talk to me. He had to discuss *everything* with me. I think after a while he got like that with Linda.

When I came to L.A., he was very happy for me, very happy. He thought it was cool that I was working as an extra on movies and getting to see all the stars. He'd ask me every night, "Oh, where you gonna be working tomorrow? Who you gonna be working with?" I was meeting different actors every day. He would send me books that these people wrote: "Oh, take the book with you and get it signed!" He was excited to hear about whatever I had done that day.

He still cared about me very much and he was definitely looking after me. He knew that I had other boyfriends—he didn't say anything about *her!* He didn't seem to mind that I had some boy living with me, ha ha ha. They would just have to be scarce whenever he came to L.A. When he came to town, all my friends went to the show, and he'd come over to the house and it was like we were still together. We *were* still together!

Johnny told me to find a house for us out here in Los Angeles. Linda didn't know anything about what was going on, and he was getting ready to leave there and come back to me. He said he was moving his money out here to California, he wanted to move out here, this is where he wanted to live. I told him I wanted to live in Silver Lake Hills so he told me to look for a house to buy.

We were getting along real well. I was having a good time out here, I had a lot of friends and I was doing a lot of things, working on myself. I'd been sober for five years and was doing very well. Sobriety from alcohol—I wasn't drinking. I was taking Xanax. He just loved it when I wasn't drinking. Johnny was so proud of me and so happy he'd start crying—he did, he would cry to me on the phone, saying that as long as I was sober we were going to be together. And he'd say, "I wish that none of that stuff woulda happened," talking about that fight that night [*the attack on Johnny in August 1983*] and all the crap I guess with Linda. But just as he started moving his money out here, I fell off the wagon and ruined everything.

⌘

In 1991 I flew to New York from LA and saw Johnny. I brought Tomahawk with me and stayed with my friend Chris Skleros again. I tried catching Johnny in his deceit—I transferred my calls to Chris's place, so he thought he was calling L.A., but he soon caught on and came over to Chris's on 46th St. Everything was fine. He told me he still had the apartment on 10th St.

I saw Gyda that trip, too, she was there, she knows Chris. She had a boyfriend at the time—Charmin, who committed suicide.

That was the year I started drinking again. I married Tom on a drunken whim on Hallowe'en. What a mistake that was. I didn't tell

Johnny for a long time. When I suggested to him once that I might marry Tom, Johnny said, "But then, who's going to marry me?"

I wanted everything to be perfect—I had money, got everything I wanted, and I still had Johnny. My ego had gotten so big and I'd gotten mean and resentful and took out a lot of shit on Tom.

I was still doing extra work and renting out myself and my S&M wardrobe and accessories to various movie sets. Then I made a fool of myself going to a studio drunk. I was so ashamed. And this actor crowd out here does *not* want to hang with someone who is on the skids. I found that out fast—they disassociated quick! And for a while there, I was wanted, in demand. My second husband David was really my downfall, but it all started with Tom.

By 1994, Tom and me were fighting a lot. Then I came home one day and he was gone; he had just packed up and left. He had gone back to Chicago.

When Tom left, I fell apart. That's when my life really started spinning out of control. I started drinking again, my insecurity got to me and I headed straight to the bar. Then I decided I had to have him back just to torture him some more. So I flew to Chicago to talk to him.

While I was there I got arrested for a DUI. I was parked! I was parked in a rental car with my dogs. The cops pulled over, came up to the car, and I'd been like, screaming—this was the next morning or something. And I had all these dogs, and they said they smelled beer on my breath. Well, the car wasn't even moving! But anyhow, they arrested me and I told them, "I don't even live here, I live in California!" Then they really wanted to keep me there and they wouldn't let me go. They had me in Cook County Jail and I had to be bailed out, Johnny had to spend a thousand bucks to bail me out of there. That was when I lost Johnny's engagement ring, too.

My brother came and picked me up at the jail. Johnny had sent him the money, so he came down to get me out of there carrying a Bible and wearing a suit, ha ha ha. Everybody thought he was a priest! I walked out and there he was, standing there reading his Bible. I was wearing these black gloves, black cape, velvet cape, some miniskirt with a pit bull on it—I don't know, I just looked really weird, and here's this guy with a Bible standing there waiting for me!

I bought a car from him and drove back to Los Angeles with this guy David, who I married on the way in Las Vegas. That was insane. He was a crackhead, cocaine, and *everywhere* we stopped on the way driving back here, all he did was score cocaine. It was just horrible. He was probably the worst drug addict I've ever been around, ha ha ha! He was a horrible husband.

I had tons of stuff in my place at that time, my mother's wedgewood dishes, furniture, all this stuff. This guy would just take whatever he wanted and go out and pawn it, you know? That was the first time I ever had to deal with anything like that. I walked in, I'm like, "Where's my camera? Where's my TV?" "I pawned it." You know? And I just *looked* at him and I could not believe that he was saying that to me! I could not believe it. I just broke down and started hysterically crying that this guy had done this, it was unbelievable to me.

I didn't stick around with him too long. I think I left him on the street, we left our apartment and everything. Johnny was paying for that apartment and he would talk to this guy sometimes. David was from Atlanta and he had this southern accent and talked to Johnny like everything was cool. He lied to Johnny about us, pretending we were fine and that he was taking care of me. He was horrible. Horrible.

*All* he wanted was to quit doing drugs—that was the most important thing in his life—*after* I allowed him to do drugs the way he really wanted to! The biggest, most incredible amount of drugs in such a short period of time! *So* much drugs, and enough money that he could do them, and he just wanted to quit. He was a quitter!

I sold a few little pieces of land in Mississippi every once in a while for extra money, like, seven, eight thousand dollars apiece. I'd get the money, and who would come running back to me? That fuckin' David! He was in a mental hospital once, he was there just to get away, he was trying to stop what he was doing. I go over there, showing money in my hand, thousands of dollars in my hand, waving at him—"Oh, look what I got!" So that he would come back! I was very lonely at the time. Very lonely. I'm not anymore, you know? No, I don't care anymore. The ones who said they loved me the most, they were the worst. Always.

By the time I was 40 I had run through all my money and I was broke, and that's when I started falling victim to the crystal meth scene. All of a sudden, all my movie connections were gone, replaced by the seamier side of L.A.—tweakers and freakers. I met a man, Michael, who would become my husband; he put the idea into my head to go into the pro dominatrix business, since I had all the equipment and accoutrements and a flair for the lifestyle. Michael was a big criminal type and a tweaker (*meth user*), like no one I had been with before. I was very intrigued. So I put an ad in the *L.A. Xpress* and the phone never stopped ringing. It was great fun for a while. I found my niche—I became Mistress Sin. "Tweak & Freak with Exotic Mistress Sin – 24/7!" That's what my ad said, and it was true, the party never stopped. The clients loved it because it took them where they really wanted to go and took away *all* their inhibitions. Michael was happy—he didn't have to worry about where his dope was coming from anymore because I always had it. I bought a lot every day and just kept going and going.

Michael was hanging out with all these crimeys and started getting busted, repeatedly. But he didn't care—I'd bail him out and he'd say, "Just another charge." All these guys I was hanging out with by this time, mind you, they've all got criminal records, they've all been to prison. All of a sudden I'm hanging out with all these fucking criminals and gang members and lowlifes, 18th Street people. I don't know what the hell happened! I was fascinated with these guys, I was just fucking off everything to hang out and do drugs with these idiots. Awful.

The last time I saw Johnny that I was still with him was probably 1995. He came over to my apartment on Cherimoya and gave some money to a friend of mine because I wasn't feeling well that day. I remember him being in that apartment. My mother was there, too. Whenever he was coming through town, he would come over to see me and see my mother. He would invite me to the show but I wouldn't go—my friends would want to go, he would get them into the show whether I went or not. I remember he was playing at, what, the Hollywood Palladium? He was playing somewhere else, too, I think, and I was trying to go see them. He was calling me. I tried to go see them, but I went on the wrong day.

I didn't know that he was already married to Linda, or that he was getting ready to move to L.A. with her. Once I started drinking after Tom left, I just couldn't stop. I was at my worst and I lost everything, including all the stuff Johnny had given me over the years, all the records, books, movies, artwork, the autographed movie star photos Johnny and I collected—everything. I am so sorry that it happened. It went on for so long. That's when he married her, I guess.

Johnny and Linda were married in 1994. The Ramones played their final shows on August 3 and 4, 1996, in Irvine CA, and August 6 in Los Angeles.

*Johnny knew for a long time that when he retired he was going to leave New York City. Last year he narrowed his choices down to*

*Orlando and Los Angeles, and finally decided on the West Coast. In May of [1996], with the help of a few friends, he loaded his possessions into an 18 wheeler and moved out of his Manhattan apartment. While the other Ramones have new musical careers in their future, Johnny doesn't ever plan on picking up a guitar again. He just wants to work on his collection of signed photos of baseball players and watch the Yankees on cable. Being in the Ramones is a job to him, and he considers himself very fortunate to have been able to make a living at it for so long. When the Ramones made their first album back in 1976, Johnny figured that was it: after it was released he would get another job doing construction and have the album to look back on. Twenty years later he can retire knowing he helped alter the course of rock music, although I don't think that's too important to him.*
— *"The Ramones" by Rick Johnson*

*I wanted to find a place where the weather was gonna be mild or nice. I would've liked it a little bit warmer here, but it's okay, I wanted to get a house. We considered Florida, Orlando, but my wife did not want to move there. If she ain't in New York she belongs here.* — *Johnny Ramone*

⌘

The last time I spoke to Johnny was the day I got arrested. I was in Phoenix. I was running from the police and moving around a lot so we hadn't spoken for a few days. Before that, I'd been telling him what was going on every day and he offered to get me out of the country even. Told me I had to get out of California, but Michael, who I was married to by then, didn't want to leave, he wouldn't leave. He got arrested before I did.

I was arrested in January of 1998 and that was when I lost touch with Johnny, the day I got arrested. That was the last time I ever spoke to him. It was unbelievable what was happening to me, you know? It just got worse and worse—like a bad movie.

I was in trouble out here in California, trying to do things, trying to get my husband Michael out of jail. I had sold some property up in Washington state and I paid $25,000 to these two lawyers to represent me and Michael. That was a lot of money! To me it was insane, but I figured if you paid these attorneys enough money, they can get you out of jail, right? And I don't know, at that point I was thinking nobody really goes to prison. I had never experienced that before. I didn't know anybody who had ever gone to prison or been in jail, except for Eliot! He's the only one in that crowd in New York that I hung out with who actually had gone to prison. And Johnny would make fun of him all the time because of that: "Ha ha, your boyfriend Eliot is in prison!" He was always doing that, laughing at people's misfortune. Horrible, it really was horrible.

Anyway, Michael had a suspended sentence to go to prison; he was really bad. He was a bad, bad guy, a criminal. And I was out on like five bails at that time and I had bounty hunters after me here in California.

So in December '97 I tried to get away, I was on the run. I ended up in Phoenix with this other guy, some idiot young kid. Then I called David, my ex-husband, for some help and he flew out to Phoenix, supposedly to help me. But all he did was look through my purse, saw $2000 in cash there—took the money and jumped in a taxi and took off back to the airport! He just came and ripped me off!

So me and the kid drove out to the airport to look for David, to get my money back. We had stopped somewhere, a truckstop, and they were selling like electric cattle prods and switchblades, ha ha ha, and I bought a bunch of this stuff! I didn't know what the fuck I was doing, I really didn't. I drove out to Phoenix in a Cadillac, then I bought another Cadillac so I had *two* Cadillacs…I had bought all these computers and printers and all this crap, and it was all in the trunk of my car. I had all this *stuff*—I don't know where the hell I thought I was going! But here I am running, and Johnny's still calling me, telling me I gotta get away.

David's in the airport, and this kid I was with walks in and pulls a switchblade on David. So the two of them are havin' a knife fight in the middle of the airport. I was outside in the car, then I went in and saw that the police had grabbed them. So I went back to the car—and the door's locked, and I don't have the key! Ha ha ha! It was a nightmare. Next thing I know, the cops are grabbing me and saying, "Do you know those guys in there?" I didn't have an ID on me because I'd destroyed all my IDs, I didn't want anybody to know who I was. The kid had been to a bar like the night before, and he ran into some girl who was selling IDs and he bought somebody else's ID for me, so that's the name I gave to these cops and that's what they booked me under. Person's name was Dawn something or other.

At that point they didn't even have my fingerprints, because I had never been arrested—except that time in New York [*1977, for dancing*] and then one time out here in California that I hadn't been charged with anything. They printed me like five times, trying to find out who the hell

I was. But I had never been in big trouble before, so they didn't even have my fingerprints or anything—I could have gotten away and they wouldn't have even known who I was.

So they're questioning the three of us. I'm not saying anything, OK? The kid is acting like he's retarded—that's what he does when he gets arrested, all of a sudden he pretends he's retarded and can't speak. And David was a really hard guy. He used to run programs for the prison systems in Atlanta. He was brilliant, he had a master's degree in psychology and he liked playing games with people, so he told the police that he was my psychiatrist and he was there to take me back to Los Angeles, to put me in a hospital or something.

So the cops think, Well, me and the kid are just *nuts*, right? So they let David go, and the cop comes in with the $2000 that David had stolen from *me* and hands it back to him! Puts it in his hands, my money! The last thing I recall is David going [*southern accent*:] "Baaaah, Daaawwn!" and waving to me as he's leaving.

I was just shaking my head looking at him and saying to myself, *You have made such a mistake*. Such a mistake. This was New Year's Eve '97 going into '98.

They held the kid, Teddy, because he had warrants there in Phoenix. His grandmother lived there so he had been back and forth. They held me until they checked me out, and they couldn't find out who the hell I was, they had no name or anything, just this fake ID that I had on me. So because I had no warrants, I had no nothing, they had to let me go. I went before the judge and they just let me go because I was not in any trouble anywhere. Meanwhile I've got bounty hunters after me in California, because of the five bails.

So they let me go. But they impounded everything, they took the car and everything that I had in the car, all the money that I had, I mean there was money hidden in the fucking car. I had like all these credit cards, there was all this shit and they took everything from me.

I didn't know where to go at that point so I ended up going to
a motel. I don't even have a car now. But I still had money on me,
so I went and bought another car! I didn't know what the fuck to do.
Meanwhile the kid's still in jail. He had to go to court, but finally his
boyfriend bailed him out. He was gay, mostly gay—all these guys
are either criminals or they're bisexual, you know, fuckin tweakers,
transsexuals, and it was just craziness. Really crazy shit.

They let Teddy out, his boyfriend bailed him out, and he
immediately flew back to Los Angeles and left me there in Phoenix by
myself. But I've still got my phone and Johnny's still got the phone
number and he's still callin' me: "What's going on? What's happening?"
I'm driving around in this Cadillac and pulling into parking lots in
shopping malls and smoking that shit—oh, and with Teddy I started
slamming it. Methamphetamine. He'd shoot me up with that crap
every day so that I can't even *think*, you know? I never did crack, I
never did cocaine. They don't do anything for me. But I'd been taking
amphetamines since I was a kid. I loved amphetamines.

So I'm all alone, driving around and hiding out in parking lots,
ducking down in the car, looking around, thinking people are following
me. I went into a shopping mall, tried to get my hair dyed to change
my appearance, ha ha ha! Just crazy shit. I'm hiding in the car, and I
swear there are people following me. I actually called the cops and said,
"There's someone on my phone," I think I even drove to the phone
company or something and told them that there were people listening
on my phone and calling me and I had to tell them about it! And they're
looking at me like I'm absolutely crazy.

So I was losing my mind there in Phoenix. I was calling David and
asking him, "Where the fuck's my two thousand dollars that you stole?"
And he's like [*southern accent*:] "Oh well, you know, when I came
back out here I had to buy myself a new *compuuuterrr*, to start up mah
*business…*" Telling me all this crap! Like *I* don't need that money for

anything! There I was, out in Phoenix, alone and absolutely *crazy*. And these guys didn't give a shit about me at all.

That idiot David basically gave me up. I used to get post office boxes all over the place to have stuff sent to. I called David asking for help, and he's like, "No, I'm not going to help you. I'm gonna help myself." But they really *were* listening in on my phone calls and now they got the phone number. And they found out where my post office box was, or something—somehow, they tracked me down to this motel.

I don't know if David was cooperating with the police. But I bet he would have, ha ha ha! He actually became sort of a cop himself afterwards. He got a job as one of those people who go out and look for people who owe money. *Those* motherfuckers. He was almost like a bounty hunter. He was making so much money, like ten or fifteen thousand dollars a week, doing this ridiculous job! He had access to anybody's information, and anyway, he knew where I was.

So the bounty hunters had found out what motel I was in, and they were on a plane out to get me. Meanwhile, there was a bounty hunter in Phoenix who came out and picked me up because they knew I had been there with Teddy. After Teddy got out, they thought he was still in Phoenix and they wanted me to help them find him. So this bounty hunter came and picked me up at the motel and we went driving around Phoenix, looking for Teddy. I was sitting there shaking, I was so nervous, I'm like sweating and shaking and we're driving around looking for Teddy. And I'm going crazy thinking, *Oh my God, they're gonna find out who I am any second and this is a game, they're just playing games with me!* We're driving around, they want me to tell them where his grandmother lived and all this stuff, and I'm just smoking cigarette after cigarette.

This motherfucker Teddy had also taken money from me before he flew back to Los Angeles. But I didn't tell them he was already gone. I didn't tell them anything. That's what you're supposed to do, you know?

After that, the bounty hunter took me back to the motel and I was nervous as a cat. By then I was sure it was playing out, that they were going to get me. At that point I had no more car anymore, I had run out of money, I just could not—I didn't even have a car to go to the bank again to take more money out. I was wiped out, I had lost everything, and I was alone in a motel room with nothing.

I'd had it. I *wanted* them to come and get me, I think. That's how I was feeling. I couldn't do anything more. I just couldn't. I was out of dope at this point, too. I'm out of dope and I don't even want to go out and look for any more.

So I decided to just let it go and I lay down on the bed. I'd already paid for this day and the next one. I just lay down and finally let myself drift off to sleep, after I'd been up for who knows how long.

Next thing I know someone's knocking on my door. I open it, and it's the bounty hunters. They've got their guns on me and everything, and they told me who they were, and I just let 'em in. I sat down, and they told me they had questioned everybody here in California that I was hanging around with, all the "Hollywood Tweakers," and some people had told them that they were gonna have to hog-tie me to take me in, because I'm *so crazy* there's no way they were going to bring me back alive! People also told them that I'd had a sex change—all these crazy stories! This is what they were telling the cops, that I'd had a sex change and I'm this desperate, crazy person, and there's no way that they can bring me back alive.

These guys also told me when they finally picked me up, they said, You know, we only have so many days to come out and find the person we're looking for. They have like 90 days or something and then that's it. They don't get paid anymore, or that's as long as you get. I only had two or three days left and then they were going to stop looking for me.

I got arrested the first week in January, maybe January 3rd, 4th, of 1998. Only a few days after David and Teddy left. Everything happened so fast, so fast. It was too much for anybody to handle in such a short period of time, it really…it was overwhelming for me.

They put their guns away, I got all my stuff together and they handcuffed me and took me back to the airport. And I was just talking with them and telling them stuff that I'd been doing. I thought they knew everything. I thought they knew *everything* about me and this whole situation. So I didn't feel like I had to disguise anything or change any of my story. But it turned out they didn't know anything! I was asking them about my husband Michael. Meanwhile Michael's out here in California, just waiting, *waiting* for them to bring me in. He was telling everybody there's no way *he's* going to prison unless *I'm* going to prison. And they also got Teddy in the meantime, so everybody's against me now. It was so horrible.

The bail bondsmen were really nice to me. They stopped and bought me beers in their car on the way out, and when we got to the airport, they took the handcuffs off me. They said, "You know, you're not as bad as they say, you're pretty nice and we're not gonna handcuff you at the airport." Because they didn't believe that I was going to run. I mean, where the hell am I going to run to? No, there's nowhere to go and I don't even want to run anymore. They even let me drink on the flight back to California. I had double bloody marys and chatted amicably with my new friends, who loved listening to my stories of sex, drugs and rock'n'roll. When we got to L.A., they let me stop at an ATM and take out $300 so I had money with me for jail. They were such gentlemen. They were just glad that the whole thing was over.

Anyway, as I'm standing there with the cops at the airport, my phone starts ringing. They let me answer, they were interested to know who it was. I guessed who it was: it was Johnny. He's like, "Tweety! Where are you, what's goin' on? Are you OK? "

And, uh…

I said to him, "Don't worry, Tweetums, I'm OK but I can't talk now," and I hung up. Then the cops took the phone and shut it off. And that was the last time I ever spoke to Johnny.

I was laughing, I think at that point I was sort of happy, relieved that it was all over. But really I was so sad, because I didn't think I'd ever see Johnny again. I didn't think I'd ever see my mother again. My mother was in California, all by herself. My brother flew out to California and picked her up.

⌘

Johnny called all my numbers but couldn't find me until finally he called my brother Richard. I had called Richard when the cops first arrived and told him what happened, just in case I didn't get to talk to Johnny before they took me in. So Richard broke the bad news: "She was arrested. The bounty hunters got her. She's in jail. She won't be getting out this time." And that was it.

I don't know what was going through Johnny's brain when he heard what had happened, but I think it must have broken his heart. I don't know. I know what *I* thought: I will always have Johnny. He's forever faithful in his love for me. He told my mother he would always take care of me. So it was a terrible shock that he never tried to contact me, never worried about me or even thought about me again after I went to prison. How could he do that to me, when he had taken care of me all my life? I didn't think Johnny would be so mean, so mean to me. I had no friends, nothing. Nobody.

I guess that was the last straw for him in my whacked-out, crazy life, and my time in prison is the time I regret the most. I don't think anyone should be able to take away a part of anyone's life, and prison does no one any good—it's just a waste of time and money and no one is taught a lesson or anything else. The girls are so frustrated and distressed that as soon as they get out, the first thing they want to do is get high and go back to the same life they had before. That's what *I* wanted to do. I wanted to catch up on all the things they had taken from me. When I was out, it always felt like I was living on borrowed time and that I was doomed to come back here sooner or later [1].

I know that Johnny could have written to me if he had wanted to, it would've been fairly easy to get my address in jail. He could have called them, or I suppose he could have asked my brother or something. He could have written to me. I believed that he was still going to send me money while I was in there and take care of me. But he didn't. And I was shocked that he didn't. He had too much of a guilty conscience to not *ever* write to me—well, he never really wrote anyway. We talked on the phone. But he sent me money all the time through the mail.

We talked all the time, every day for so many years. I thought we were so close as friends and that I knew him so well. He told me everything—well, not *everything*, but he told me what was going on in his life and I told him what was going on in mine. Except, you know, we didn't talk about *her*. Just like we didn't talk really about my boyfriends, other than I lived with so-and-so and they would answer the phone, *Oh hi!* He would talk to them and ask them how I was doing and blah blah blah, do I have what I need, you know. He got to be friendly with a couple of them.

I don't know what happened. Maybe it became too complicated for him to stay in touch once I was in prison, or maybe Linda found out and put a stop to it. She might have said to him, Either you stop talking to her or whatever, communicating with her, or I'm going to leave, and he wouldn't want that. Because then he would be alone. Now, I heard somewhere that at some point she said she wanted to get back with Joey.

This is what I've heard. She probably was just saying that, but Joey I think probably treated her a little bit more special. She seemed to mean a lot to Joey. And Johnny might have bought her things, but I'm sure Joey would have, too.

I just know that he didn't like to be alone, he was afraid to be alone. And he *wasn't* alone—but if I hadn't gone to prison, our relationship would have continued, even if I was in the position of being the one that's hidden, the one he's having an affair with. Then all of a sudden I'm in prison and he's not seeing me, he's not able to call me. When he had been calling me every single day, every day I was away from him, when he supposedly was with Linda. And telling me he didn't feel right if he couldn't talk to me every day—that he needed that to normalize his life. He enjoyed talking to me and getting my input on everything. I don't know if she knows that or not.

⌘

My husband Michael and I both went to prison, but I got a much heavier sentence and he got out way before me. They gave me four and a half, five years almost. First time I'm going in—five years. After I paid all that money to the lawyers and everything! That was the start of my education in the "Big House." Michael had a three-year joint suspension, he ended up getting two years, he was out in like a year—I got all the time. Michael couldn't believe that I got all those years. He was being so mean to me, he just wanted me caught, he wanted me going to prison, too. But then later on, he said to me, "Oh, wow, when I heard what happened I felt really bad!"

Michael left me while I was in prison. We got in a fight on the phone and he stopped writing to me all of a sudden. He started sending all my letters back and wouldn't take my phone calls, he changed the phone number. And I was having a nervous breakdown because of this. I was alone in there every day, just thinking, *Where is he?* Then I found out he had met some other girl and he had her move in while I was in prison.

*And where's Johnny? Why doesn't he write to me? Who is he with? How can he not call me or send me any money?* I just sat there every day. I was going absolutely crazy. I had never been alone like that, never. I had nobody. I had nothing, I had no money anymore. I was totally alone. I had never been on my own and I was so lonely. I wrote to Johnny wherever I could, but I really didn't know where I should write to him. I mean, I tried to write to him on 10th Street, obviously he was gone from 10th Street—I tried writing to him I think at Sire Records, but the Ramones weren't with them anymore. I didn't know what record company or who their manager was anymore, it wasn't who it used to be and I didn't know where I could find him. Later on, I wrote directly to his house on Deervale, but I don't know if he ever got any of those letters.

It's hard to believe how much time I wasted waiting for Johnny, thinking everything would be fine and we'd be together again. I hung around with men who were never good enough, who could never take his place. I wanted guys I would have no problem getting rid of at a moment's notice in case Johnny came back suddenly. So I let myself down and every relationship I had was doomed from the start. There was no real love. I ran their lives, I used them for sex and companionship, and I looked down on them because I used them and they were nothing. And I took care of them all with Johnny's money! As well as a lot of money of my own that I had gone through by 1996 or so. I was a very empty, lonely woman.

Up until that point, if I ever needed anything, all I had to do was call my mother or call Johnny. I never had to do a damn thing, I never had

to work, I never had to do *anything*. Until I was forty years old! I had
a great life for forty years! You know, and I should be happy about it. I
don't know what happened the last eighteen, though! I guess everyone
has their ups and downs, but my downs took me down pretty hard and
that was the end of the ride for me, after forty years.

> Johnny Ramone was diagnosed with
> prostate cancer in Spring 1998, shortly after
> Roxy was arrested, and started radiation
> treatments in July.

The day I got out of prison in 2001, my brother came to pick me up
and my husband Michael was calling me, he wanted me to come over
to see him and his new girlfriend. I went the next day, and he sat me
down and told me that he was HIV positive and he wanted to be with
somebody who was also HIV positive, that he never wanted to hurt me.
And I said, "Well, why didn't you tell me that, instead of driving me
crazy in there?"

My husband before him had HIV, too—I never got it. Maybe I'm a
missing link or something, I don't know, but I didn't get it. But I didn't
care, I really didn't care. I wanted to be with Michael. I moved back in
with him and I worked every day. I was still in love with him. I took care
of him. I just wanted to be with him.

And I had nothing. I'd been in prison for four years and you know,
you go away and all your stuff, which I had a house full of, disappears
and you have to start over.

Michael was my favorite husband. He was a lot of fun. He was a criminal and he just didn't give a fuck about anything, you know? He got me into doing criminal things. He was a bisexual swish and very protective, I mean jealous—he liked to fight! People were afraid of him. He reminded my mother of my father. Michael was very handsome, he looked like a model when I met him. He'd been a hustler, a male hustler.

But after I moved back in with him everything started happening again. It was so easy to just fall back into my Mistress persona, and all that went with it, the drugs and all the rest. I was well-known in the BDSM community and in demand, and all I had to do was put up an ad on the internet and start the party up again. We started making a lot of money again—well, *I* did! But I felt like I was living on borrowed time and that I was bound to get busted sooner or later, so just have a good time and accumulate as much as I could, as fast as I could.

Then he started doing criminal shit again. He broke my collarbone and a bunch of other shit. Finally we both went back to prison. When I got out again, I met somebody else and moved to Beverly Hills with him. Michael got out and started stalking me over there. Then he just disappeared. He went to Boston, or somewhere in Connecticut. I don't know what happened to him.

# 2003–04

I WAS IN PRISON IN '98, '99, 2000, and pretty much all of 2001. When I finally got to see Johnny again it was 2003. He was with Rob Zombie at Tower Records signing a record that had just come out.

> The in-store signing session for the Ramones tribute CD, *We're a Happy Family* (Columbia), took place at Tower Records on Sunset Boulevard, Hollywood CA on Tuesday, February 11, 2003, the day of the record's release; with Johnny Ramone, Rob Zombie and Pete Yorn.

He was standing there, wearing glasses—little reading glasses. He was talking to everybody as usual, and then he looked over and he saw me. I was in line to talk to him, I didn't want to barge up there or anything. But when he saw me, he just sorta shook his head and went, "*Ahh, man!*"

I remember it so clearly. I had dressed up and thought I looked good. I had my camcorder and I was taking some pictures. I thought for sure we would talk! Just go up and talk to him. I was standing in the line for a long time, it was at the end, and if I'd just stayed in line and kept going, I could have talked to him. But I kept letting people ahead of me. Because I didn't have an album for him to sign, I figured I would let all these people go ahead. I should have just stayed in that line and kept going!

Then one of the girls that worked there showed up and said, "OK, that's it for autographs," everybody's gotta go. I said, "No, I'm here to talk to him, I know him." And they said, "Oh no, you gotta go," and they made me leave. What the fuck? I don't know if somebody told them to do that or what, but it was so humiliating and so heartbreaking.

It never even occurred to me that he wouldn't talk to me. *Never*— you know? How could he? I mean, it was just so bizarre. Nobody knows each other intimately for 20 years, then just ignores them. There was something else going on.

I don't think he was scared of me or anything like that. He didn't look like he was scared of me! He looked me in the eye and he put his head down and shook his head, like, *Oh, no! No no no. What's she doing here? No no no no no...* Like, what the fuck, after all this time?

He snubbed me like I was an annoying fan or something. He never should have done that. I couldn't believe that he did that. Michael had brought me out there and he even went and talked to him, trying to figure out if there was any problem. Michael walked right up, he didn't stand in any line, he just went right over to Johnny and said, "Hey, Cynthia is here, she wants to talk to you." Then he went outside and I stayed inside by myself, and just let everybody go ahead of me and stood there and didn't say anything.

Maybe it was because he was there with Rob Zombie and he's friends with Linda, and Johnny was scared that it would get back to her, but still, I did not expect that reaction. Even when he ran into his ex-wife on the subway, he stopped and talked to her. He loved me *for years!!* What was the meaning of that shake of his head? I thought he was just kidding with that. I thought for sure he would talk to me, that's why I waited around for so long on the side until he was done with all his fans, like I would normally do. I waited.

So I stood there and stood there, and finally they left, and I didn't get to talk to him. I went out and got in the car with Michael and he said, "What happened?" and I said, "He just left." And he was like, "Oh no, you've gotta talk to him." Michael, my very tough fifth husband— even his heart broke at the way Johnny treated me. *He* was there when Johnny was calling all the time! *My first, second, third, fourth and fifth husbands* all *spoke with Johnny!* He could not understand why this guy would do this to me, and he was all pissed off that Johnny didn't stay and talk to me, after it had been so many years that I had been in prison and everything, and looking for him, and then Michael had found out that he was going to be at Tower Records that night. He was not going to let him get away with this.

So we waited until they left, Johnny got in some limousine, and we started following him. We were driving after his car, Michael and I. "Make sure you talk to him." We followed him for a while, to Beverly Hills, but finally I just said, "Oh forget it, you know, I don't even want to." He's like running away from me. I told Michael to stop, it was ridiculous. What was I gonna do? I mean, we could have continued, but I'm sure it would have just caused some sort of scene somehow. I was miserable and bewildered, but still I figured I would see him again. We were too close to ever not speak to each other again.

I never thought he would do that to me. But then I didn't know that he was married, either, or any of that other crap! I thought he would be very happy to see me.

You don't do that! After knowing someone all your life! It's like he was my dad, and all of a sudden he doesn't want to talk to me? Basically that's how I felt—like my father was gone. He *acted* like my dad, he took care of me all those years. But to shake his head and look down and walk away from me without saying a word, and my husband has to go up and say, "Johnny, Cynthia wants to talk to you, she's right here, y'know, you gotta talk to her"—and he just goes and gets in his fuckin' little car and rides off without even saying anything to me? How could he? *How could he?* Why, is somebody going to tell *Linda?* Of course, that's what he was afraid of, I'm sure. Unless he had just gotten that rotten that he just didn't give a fuck about anybody anymore.

When I got back to the house, I realized that the camcorder battery had run down so there were only a few seconds of Johnny, but I cherished those seconds even though they broke my heart.

After all these years, that moment still haunts me. Did he already know he was sick at the time? Was he sparing me the agony of going through that with him? He knew how sensitive and shy I was. Why would he do that? He wasn't a heartless person. I wish someone could tell me how he felt about me at that time.

In early 2003, Johnny Ramone started chemotherapy treatment at Cedars-Sinai Medical Center in L.A.

*"Once every few weeks, I pick up the guitar for five minutes to strum around. It would be embarrassing to continue playing those songs. Unless you can get that same response, and be as good as we were, there's no point to it." He never wanted to be onstage past his prime. "I would have stopped in 1980 if I could have afforded to," he said. "I was looking to do it for five years, become the*

*biggest band in the world, and stop. That was*
*my goal. I was a failure."*    — *Johnny Ramone*

Johnny always wanted a Chevy—a '57 Chevy Bel Aire, painted blue. Blue and white. That was going to be the car that he bought out in California. Well, this is the place to get that car. But no, he never did. I don't know why.

**He did, however, own a turquoise and**
**white 1958 Ford Fairlane when he lived**
**in New York in the 1990s.**

He was going to get that car, and grow a beard, and be bald with his pot belly. He didn't want to have to shave anymore. He had to shave a lot, ha ha ha! He always had 5 o'clock shadow, and he wanted to look good. So he said once this was over he was gonna grow a long beard and not have to shave anymore.

I never got to see where he lived. I wanted to drive by, take a look, but I never did.

**Johnny Ramone died in his sleep at his home**
**in Sherman Oaks, California, on Wednesday**
**afternoon, September 15, 2004.**

How could I have been in a rehab when he was dying? I was at Cri-Help when it happened. I tried to see him, I went to that last concert. I snuck out with two other girls from the rehab, but he didn't show up. [*September 12, 2004: Ramones 30th anniversary tribute concert in L.A., three days before Johnny died.*] I saw Danny [*Fields*], Phil Spector's bodyguards, Jenny Lens, Arturo, Monte, but I couldn't get in. I had no ticket and Monte wouldn't let me in. I should have tried harder to see him and talk to him instead of what I was doing. I feel so bad. I never saw an end like that—so sudden, so quick, so soon.

I taught him a lot of things, you know? He would ask me what I thought he should collect, and I would tell him, "Oh, I think that this would be a good thing to collect." We planned, we planned what we were going to do. Yeah, someday we're gonna have all these collections! And get old in Florida, and he'd shave his head...Shave his head, and grow a beard, and have his parking lot.

I wish I had just been able to speak with him before he died. That would have put to rest a lot of unanswered questions, and my heart would not hurt so bad now when I think about him. I just can't see him changing that much, that he wouldn't want to talk to me. I will never believe it or understand it.

⌘

Sometimes I think I self-destructed because it was the only way Johnny would let me go, and the only way I could get beyond it all and obliterate what we had. I pushed him away until I finally disappeared. We were going our separate ways, especially after he moved to Los Angeles and all those celebrities started fawning around him. Before, when Johnny was punk rock, we didn't fit in with Studio 54 patrons. Before Linda, that is. But after he got with her, it seemed like his social calendar revolved around events he once delighted in jeering at.

Maybe I wasn't the right person for the job. I went in a different direction—a darker direction. What would have happened if I hadn't? Would things have gone along the way they always did, him leading the double life? Or would he have dumped her and come back to me? Who's to know.

I gave him a way out, not very gracefully for myself. I destroyed myself in the process and still have not been able to crawl out of this hole completely. I wanted to destroy myself and the pain I couldn't bear. The only things that gave me any sense of fulfillment were drugs and dominatrixing, especially after I couldn't work in movies anymore. I know it tormented him that I left him for drugs and alcohol and I regret it now. I guess being a dominatrix and a drug addict became glamorous for me, like his life did for him, but the drugs ruined me. At the time, I felt like drinking and drugs helped me get over my shyness and low self-esteem, and deal with my sexuality, but I forfeited my security and happiness.

Sometimes I can see so clearly how I sabotaged my whole life and everything good I had, and I really hate myself. I get so down on myself and wish I could live it over or do something about it. If I could do it all again, I would leave the drugs and alcohol out. What a different life I would have had. I was a little off in my judgment, but I need to redeem myself somehow. I don't want to be remembered as a drug addict or a drunk. I need to get sober and *like it!* No matter what, I have to do something different this time, take a different path and come up with some happiness, somehow.

Johnny was way out of his league when I really started with the drugs. He wouldn't have known what to do. In the end, he would have been too weary to do anything about me. Nor would I have known what to do with the pain of his dying. I had become a tremendous bother to him and I hate being a bother to anyone. I'd rather go off and be a bother by myself. I had become bitterly disappointed in my life with Johnny and I hated Linda for stepping into my shoes. He told me *he* hated her. Then why did he continue with her?

And why did Johnny continue with *me* if he was so in love with Linda? Because he wasn't. He called me every day, even when he was with her. What does that tell you? He was too scared to commit to her until I was completely gone, out of the picture. Linda has the CDCR to thank for sealing it with Johnny. He spoke badly of her every time I brought her up, always told me he loved me and wished things had been different, and he would cry. Johnny was all twisted in his thinking. He seemed pretty miserable at times. It was his own doing, though—his double life that he always had to have. I didn't help with my binge drinking. But Linda would have faded out sooner or later, I'm sure she would have tired of it all and moved on to someone else's boyfriend.

People think I put him through such hell. They don't know what he did to me, and the hell I went through, and still do. It all almost killed me. But I'm the one still alive. I didn't make all the trouble—Linda did. They caused me a lot of anguish. I still cry. People never cared how miserable I was. No one even knew. No one was close to John then, so they weren't close to me, nor were they allowed to be. I guess everyone expected me to die. But I didn't. Karma's a bitch, you know? I was there, and I'm still here!

I should have tried harder. I wish I could have at least had a few words with him without him being afraid of the bitch finding out. Too late now. He's not around to set things straight. I hate being cast as a pathetic drunk, a crazy person who ended up where she belonged. I hate being the victim, which is what I am. I hate being dismissed and forgotten. I've stopped being human to people when they hear that I'm crazy and no good. And I end up with nothing, while she ended up with it all. I don't even have a place to live, and I know that's not what he would have wanted. Cruel. Crazy. I was left out in the cold after I had been through so much with him, with all of them.

What really sticks in my mind are all the times he cried, really cried. How very sensitive he was, and how sentimental, like at Christmas. That one Christmas when I worked at Macy's and bought him all those presents with my pay, and him saying, "This is my best Christmas ever!" He used to say Christmas and birthdays are just for kids and try to ignore them, especially after his father died, but that was because he was so sentimental.

There were two sides to Johnny, at least—I saw them all. He let me inside. It was very hard to get inside. That's why I can't believe he would ever shut me out. He told me everything and I had been there through the years, all the ups and downs. And I always thought he would be around. His death was so unexpected, so hard.

I dream about him a lot. I wish to God I could just have spoken to him once before he went. In my dreams I do, all the time, and I feel like he's trying to make up for what happened, and that he does love me still, tremendously, as I do him. He said he'd always love me and take care of me and I believed him—I believe him still and I still believe he was my soul mate.

He was the great love of my life. My first true love.

⌘

Johnny didn't like death. He didn't like to be around people that were sick or dying, like when Anya was dying, he didn't want to be around her. "Ha ha, Anya's got cancer! Why are you crying, you knew she was gonna die! Ha ha!" Just *mean!* Mean things like that. And when Joey was dying, he wouldn't even talk to him. A simple apology would have been nice—an acknowledgement. That's all I wanted, too. I don't understand why he would be so mean like that. I hope that when he was dying, people didn't do that to him.

It's funny, I wonder when he was sick, after he found out he had cancer, did he not want people around? I don't know. I guess he wanted his new celebrity friends around him. I heard he wouldn't let Tommy come and see him before he died, but he let all those fuckin' people that he had just *met* come over. How could he have not let somebody like Tommy or somebody in the band come over to see him? [1]

Celebrity friends. Celebrity friends. He didn't have any celebrity friends in New York. We never hung out with any people like that while we were together, ever. He didn't want to! He didn't like anybody who was in another band. At that time, he didn't want to be around anybody who was in a band. He didn't like those people. The only people that he seemed to *like* were dead actors and baseball players!

And I think he was hanging around with Linda because she was as mean as he could be! I see pictures of her with that fuckin' stone face, *never* a smile, nothing. With those goddamn outfits on, those Elvis throwaways that she wears, and that stone face that doesn't crack a smile. She knows nothing about anything that Johnny and I were interested in. She knows nothing.

*Pete Yorn, John Frusciante and Eddie Vedder (with his baby girl, Olivia, in tow) also spoke, but Vincent Gallo gave a truly Galloesque eulogy, spending more time discussing*

*himself than Johnny and letting everyone
know that he only befriended Johnny because
he liked Linda. "I knew to be Linda's friend I
had to be friends with Johnny, and he seemed
so crotchety and mean and nasty. I'm more
avant-garde than Johnny. Of course, I liked
the Ramones, but I was more into more
arty bands. It wasn't like I needed to meet
Johnny Ramone. I would have preferred the
guitar player for Magazine or Ultravox or
something." — LA Weekly*

You know, I watched that movie *Too Tough To Die* the other
night. [Too Tough to Die: A Tribute to Johnny Ramone (2006) *is the
documentary film of the Ramones' 30th anniversary concert in Los
Angeles on September 12, 2004.*] Oh man, I didn't want to! When it
came on I was like, I don't even wanna watch this! Because I know it's
going to make me feel bad or angry or *something*, I just knew something
was going to piss me off so bad or make me cry or something like that.
Anyhow, it wasn't as bad as I thought it would be, it was just stupid. All
those fuckin' motherfuckers getting up and talking about him, how great
he was and this and that—none of these people are for real! I mean, does
anybody really think that?

*Nobody* liked him! He had no friends! For years, he was like the
biggest asshole around! *Nobody liked him*. Nobody in New York liked
him. Nobody! He was an asshole. He called *me* an asshole in front of
people. He hit me in front of other people. People have seen this.

Then he's with Linda and they're running around Hollywood and
I don't know what the fuck! Did you ever see that one interview with

her, when she was saying, "Oh when we moved out here—you gotta be *rich!* People look at you and they see how much money you've got and you gotta act like you got money"—did you hear her say that shit? Unbelievable! That she would act like that on television. If I was married to him and he died like that, I would not even *appear* on television. I wouldn't be saying anything to anybody, especially something stupid like that.

> *You live in New York, it isn't as—it isn't such a big deal, 'cause people walk around and no one shows their wealth, and no one really—you know, everyone gets in a cab, everyone lives in an apartment. In LA it's kind of, everyone has a big house, everyone has a nice car and you see really what goes on. And kind of everyone knows how much you're worth just walking down the street. ... But I'll tell you one thing: the weather's nice.*
> — *Linda Ramone*

And the way she got into it with his mother right after he died, about money...It was too painful, I could not—I didn't want to see anything like that, for years I didn't want to see any of it. I didn't want to know anything about it. I've heard about it now. I've heard how she wouldn't let his mother have any money [2].

Apparently she wouldn't let him give money to Rosana or me when he wanted to, either. Vera told me this. She told me that John and Linda came to Florida once, and Vera and her husband went to Disney World with them. That's when Vera learned that John wanted to leave both me and Rosana some money, but Linda refused to let him do this.

And I would believe that. I think he would have wanted to make things right before he died. I hope it's true—it would make me feel a whole hell of a lot better if it *was* true. I know he was in touch with Rosana because she forwarded me an email that Johnny sent her right before he died. Pictures of his house out here in California. There's a picture of his swimming pool, and a picture of him with a bunch of pictures behind him. I guess he got her email and sent them to her. Show her how good he was doing or whatever.

Then again, Vera also believed that someone put a curse on the Ramones, so who knows! John would actually say that a lot. He didn't like shaking hands or taking anything from anyone for fear of germs. If someone tried to pass him something, he would always say, "What are you trying to pass me? A curse?" I still say that to this day! It was a joke. Dee Dee OD'd, Joey was always frail and sick, and John was mean and would not ever go to a doctor for anything. That's why they all died young. [3]

# 2010

*Rob Zombie explained how the statue came to be. "One of Johnny's favorite things to do was to keep reminding Linda what a lucky woman she was to be living with a legend. [Impersonating Johnny] 'Linda, I'm a fuckin' legend. You're living in the lap of luxury because of me. Without me, you're nothing.' So I thought I'd have my friend Wayne [Toth] sculpt an award that just said, 'Legend.' One day we were talking—and at this point Johnny was very sick—we sort of talked about what was inevitably going to happen and about having some sort of headstone or memorial, and I said, 'Johnny, why don't you make a giant-sized one of this fucking thing as a joke?' And now that joke is sitting over there, weighs 50,000 pounds, and it's made out of bronze." — LA Weekly*

EVENTUALLY I SAW HER. I saw her at the cemetery. Yeah, me and my boyfriend at the time and this other guy, we went to the cemetery that night for the thing [*the Hollywood Forever Cemetery, where Johnny's memorial stone is located, and where Linda Ramone hosts a birthday*

*tribute and movie screening each year*]. She had it on her birthday that
year. Her birthday is July 26, if I remember. [*The 2010 tribute was held
on Sunday, July 25.*] I know she's a Leo, and I know it was the end of
July, it was the 26th or the 28th—1958. That's her birthday. It's funny
how you remember some things. It was nowhere near Johnny's birthday.

So she had Johnny's birthday tribute on her birthday. It doesn't
really feel like she cares about Johnny that much. She always was about
herself, and elevating herself wherever she could. Anyhow, I saw Tommy
[*Ramone*] there and I went over and talked, and that was cool. He seemed
happy to see me, which was nice. And then towards the end we went
and we saw Johnny's supposed gravesite—the memorial statue. I wish it
really was his gravesite. Johnny always told me he wanted to be buried in
a mausoleum, above the ground. He never wanted to be cremated.

Who else has a statue like that, John Wayne? Ha ha ha! I think John
Wayne has a statue like that. And that quote, that's somebody else's
quote. Johnny didn't say that himself! I know that quote. Somebody else
said that, some actor I think [1].

So we go over and look at the s tatue, and then some people came
over and took some pictures of me and Tommy. I was cute, I was wearing
this little party dress. Towards the end, I was just feeling like there was
something I was supposed to do, I was there for a reason. *Oh yeah, you
know what? I gotta go over and say something to that bitch. I gotta go
say hi.*

She wasn't circulating around but I knew where she was: she was in
the little backstage part, the VIP section that was roped off. The two guys
I was with have gone to the car, they're bored already—stayed there long
enough, let's get out of here. But I'm still running around, so I went back
by the rope where I figured Linda would be.

And then she comes out, wearing that same tired white fake fur
and the big glasses and the spiky boots. She's got all these different
outfits that all look the same. What *is* that look? I mean, what are those

costumes that she wears? She looks like she's wearing something Elvis might have thrown away! And she actually goes around saying that she has all of her clothes made for her. They're custom made, they're all custom made. What, you can't walk into a store and buy something that makes you look like a clown—you have to have it *made* for you?

Anyway, I was standing there and I saw her, and I went, "Linda! Hey, Linda!" And she turns around and she *loooooks*—and she lifts her glasses up, and she *loooooks* again, closer—And then her face changes, all of a sudden she gets this look of shock, and then *horror!* Like, *Oh my God!* Ha ha ha! She was with that tall, geeky boyfriend of hers, JD something. [*L.A. musician JD King*] And some other tall guy. Then she talked to the security, and then some woman security guard comes walking up to me, asking me questions, "Do you know her? What are you doing here?" Asking me why I was standing there, in that spot. I'm just standin' here and watchin' a movie, whatever! Obviously Linda had sent her over to talk to me and try to tell me to leave.

But Linda herself wouldn't say anything to me. Once she realized who I was, all of a sudden she went into shock and horror. And then sent security over. Why do that? I mean, if *I* had stolen somebody's boyfriend and all of a sudden they showed up years later, and I was married to the guy or whatever—if she wants to talk to me, you know what, I'm gonna go up to her and I'm gonna talk to her. I would've given her that much. Right? Let's just get this over with and maybe we can be friends. Whatever.

But no. She didn't do that. She tried to make me feel like I was out of place or something, which I totally wasn't.

She looked like she'd a ghost, but I don't think she was scared of me. Why would she be? Because I had been in and out of prison? How would she know that? I don't think John even knew that. He knew that I went the first time, but I doubt he would have talked to her about it. And I don't know what he thought after that, because he stopped talking to me and I had no place to write to him. We were not in touch anymore.

Johnny could not be alone. He didn't know how to be alone. He would never leave anybody until he knew there was somebody else, and then he tried to hang on to the other person as well. He never wanted to give anyone up. Hanging on and hanging on forever, if he could. If I hadn't gone away, I'm sure that we would have had a relationship till the day he died. As it was, she never found out about it. I hadn't lived in New York for a number of years and it was still going on and she didn't know about it. He and I spoke to each other every day, many times a day, and he paid for everything for me. And he made plans with me for the future. And he lied about her, too, told me he wasn't seeing her! Told me he hated her. He made it seem like there was nothing going on between them, always.

But finally he had to let me go because I was gone. I couldn't be there for him anymore, not even to talk to. Even when he was living with his wife [*Rosana*], he would go out—"Oh I gotta go out for a quart of milk," I gotta do this, I gotta run out, let me do something for you, let me go outside for a minute—so he could call me! You know? We'd have that connection.

See, I didn't need to be around him every second, like Linda did. But when I went to prison, I was cut off from him and I was going to be for a number of years. What was he gonna do? As I say, he couldn't be alone. He had never been alone in his life and he was incapable of being alone, he always needed somebody. And apparently not just *one* somebody! He would never leave her unless he had me or somebody else to go to. So that was it.

Even before that, I don't think he was afraid of me because I went to prison. He sent me money to keep me out of there. He told me to flee the country, he would've sent me money to do that if I'd wanted it! I had been arrested before and he bailed me out. He bailed me out in Chicago, he sent me a thousand dollars and bailed me out of jail there. And I was in jail for five months in '97. He knew how I was living. But then all of a sudden he was completely cut off from me. And he had all those secrets.

# 2011

I SAW *END OF THE CENTURY* for the first time a couple of days ago.
I thought the more touchy subjects could've been, uh—touched upon!
Ha ha ha! But again, nothing was really said. It made me a little sad, but
I thought it would be worse. I thought there would be a little bit more to
it. But there were no new revelations or anything like that. At least not to  .
me. And Johnny didn't actually talk about anything, because Linda was
standing right there! They have her talking off-camera about Joey, and
I could see that Johnny was upset. But then he did something that was a
little strange:  he just shut up. If I had done something like that, he'd say,
"What the fuck do you know, asshole?" But then, I wouldn't be standing
there listening.

He doesn't discuss the situation at all. He didn't want to and that
was that. He did not want to talk about it, my guess is, because it was a
little too fresh and he probably was afraid that I was going to see that.
Even in '97, we were still pretty much—you know, he was paying for
everything of mine and he was still communicating with me.

The only way the documentary filmmakers could
secure Joey's participation was if Johnny agreed
to talk about the Linda situation. But in the film,
the story is actually told by other people; Johnny
himself says nothing about it. *End of the Century*

was released in 2004, but most of the interviews,
including the one where Johnny is asked about
the falling-out with Joey over Linda, were filmed
in the late 1990s or early 2000s.

And I was looking at that book that Joey's brother wrote—Mitch's book [Mickey Leigh's 2010 memoir, *I Slept With Joey Ramone*]. It really touched my heart that he included me in the acknowledgements— someone *did* remember! And Mitch married Arlene? And he's still married to her? Wow! I thought he was going to marry her, but I thought by now he was probably married to somebody else or something.

That's great, you know? They were all pretty loyal, they stuck with who they were with, all of 'em. Claudia and Tommy, and Dee Dee and Vera were together a long time, until she couldn't take it anymore... and Marc and Marion, they've been together forever. And I think we would have stayed together, too—of course we would've. If that didn't happen.

# Epilogue: Dominatrix

I GOT ALL MY ADS UP FINALLY and now I'm so busy I'm just exhausted. I'm teaching girls who want to do what I do, teaching them how to do it. It's a real skill and it's very psychological; I am not actually a violent person!

But there is a lot of skill involved. There's technical skill—you have to know how not to kill someone, you really do. Some of these young girls, they don't know what they're doing, they could hurt these guys, and some of them *want* to hurt them. That's not the point. When I was in treatment, I remember hearing that someone was killed in a dungeon, by a dominatrix. I don't know if he wanted to be killed or if the girl wanted to kill him, but that happened [1].

I'm always really careful with these guys. I know how many minutes they should be wrapped up or have their feet up or whatever, because I've read about it and I've studied it. But you have to be really careful.

It is legal, however, because there's no exchange of money for sexual favors. The payment is a donation—tribute. The police don't fuck with the dominatrixes. Remember the Craigslist Killer? When the cops were tracking him, they used to go on Craigslist and try to bust people, but they never screwed around with the dominatrixes, just the hookers. Because we're not supposed to have sex with any of these people. If you're a true dominatrix, you don't do that. It's a mind fuck, it's all psychological. These guys don't want to have sex. If they're truly a submissive type, they don't want that—they don't want to ruin that illusion and that fantasy. And that's what would do it.

I didn't call myself a domme until I'd had 20 years of practice and experience in the lifestyle, and then another eight years before I went pro. Since age 14, it's been my life. It started with my first drug-dealing, drop-out boyfriend. He was also a heroin addict and was very physically and sexually abusive. Everyone would say "How can you take it?" and "Why don't you get away from him?" But I loved it. It gave me a purpose and an identity. That was my first taste of the S&M lifestyle— and I was hooked. I didn't know at the time that it had a name and that there was a whole world associated with it, but I knew I wanted to explore my sexuality and what sado-masochistic relationships involved.

Eventually I found the book *The Story of O*, by Pauline Reáge. I was fascinated by the BDSM community, which was was very hush-hush and underground in the 1970s. Pauline Reáge's book also influenced Anne Rice, whose *Sleeping Beauty* series years later made sado-masochism and its fantasies and fetishes more available to the mainstream.

The S&M clothing and attitude also fit in with the punk rock revolution that was happening in New York and London, and I found myself at the center of that scene even before I got together with Johnny. I started acquiring a vast wardrobe of bondage and fetish clothing which I wore daily. Vinyl, leather and latex became my mainstays, and dressing this way made me feel wonderfully sexy and at home in my own skin.

Johnny, without knowing it, was my dream master. Prone to sadistic jealous rages and total control. I was the perfect sub, giving myself, even sacrificing myself for him and our relationship. I didn't say a thing for a long time when I should have. I had blatant evidence of his cheating but I couldn't and wouldn't believe it. He was my father/lover/master. Even when we wouldn't have sex but once a month because of his herpes, I tried not to rock the boat or say anything. I was secure in my situation and wanted to stay that way. After he was beaten up in 1983, everything changed, but he still needed me almost till the end. We lost touch when I went to prison, and had been out of contact for six years when he died in

2004.

With Anya, I was the one who was into the S&M lifestyle. She was a disco girl when I met her, I introduced her to it. I was a submissive but was into any S&M scenes I could find. I was into heavy bondage, floggings and pain, I liked to be hurt and bruises left. My friends didn't understand it, but Anya liked it when I had her do a scene with me for the owner of one of the clubs where we used to dance. I told her to dominate me. She got into it. Anya was a natural domme. She loved to inflict pain on men as well as women. We would go to his place afterwards and she'd whip me and make me suck his cock while she stuffed pills in my mouth and coke up my nose. I didn't mind. It was sensual and kinky and then I'd be ready to go to Max's and find a nice young victim of my own!

I would eventually grow into being the domme Mistress Sin, but I felt you had to be the sub first, so you would know both sides of the coin. Maybe I'm wrong, but it seems like a progression to me. But once you're known as a dominatrix, you are always the one in charge. You don't switch. Some of the girls who work in these dungeons do—"Oh, I'm a switch"—No. You have to be one or the other, because the guys will get a picture of you as this person, and that becomes part of the fantasy.

You have to have trust with your clients. I know the guys who are coming over to see me. They all have, most of them have power, they've got money, they've got a good job, and they have sought me out. They want to come over and relax and let someone else take charge for a while. Or else they want to do something that they can't do at home, that they can't do with their wife or their girlfriend. The wife doesn't wanna know about it, they don't wanna hear about it—"Go get somebody else to do that, because I don't want to." But they don't want to get a divorce, either. So the men come over and see me. It's like being a family therapist. I keep marriages together, you know? I'm a specialist in a certain field of sexuality.

And because of this, I'm not putting myself in danger. These guys

don't want anything from me, they don't want to rob me. I've only had
I think two occasions where I even had to call someone else in. Usually
that never happens.

There was one time I needed money really bad, and this guy called
up and asked if there were any submissive girls. So somebody else was
going to come over and be a submissive for this guy and give me half
the money, but she didn't show up. So I figured I better do it myself!
I've never had to work in a place where I was alone, first of all, because
I always lived with somebody. There were always guys there, just in
case anything happened, but nothing ever did. Anyhow, this guy came
over and my boyfriend wasn't home at the time. He came up and I don't
know, he wanted to do something and I went along with it for a while,
and then he started getting on my nerves. It was getting a little peculiar,
stepping over that line. And I just went nuts all of a sudden and my
boyfriend had some guns in the house. So I pulled out a gun and pointed
it at him. He thought it was part of the therapy—part of the act! And he
went, "No, no, wait a second, wait a second, this is a little bit too rough
for me. I'm gonna go now!" And then I was like, "No. *I* wanna play.
You're not goin' anywhere!" Ha ha ha. So that's one time that I resorted
to something like that.

And the other time I was really, really tired and I was waiting up for
this guy who drove down from Ventura, which was a long way. When
he got there, it was like four o'clock in the morning and I said, OK,
well, where's the money? And he said, "Oh, I couldn't get the money, I
can't get it till the bank opens in the morning." I said, Forget it, I don't
want to do this now, but he would not leave. Then he smacked my ass or
something, and that was it. I had to call my husband in: "Michael, this
guy's annoying me!" My husband was just waiting, *waiting* to come in
and do something to these guys! He loved to fight. He was a badass. He
used to walk around wearing leather overalls with no shirt underneath,
and a black leather hood, and walk by with a chainsaw or something! Ha

ha ha! So he looked dangerous. He looked totally *nuts!* Anyway, he got
rid of that guy real quick. So no, there were not any problems. I mean,
those are very minor problems.

Sometimes men want the dominatrix to demand money from them
or demand presents or blackmail them into giving them money. That's
financial domination, or money slaves. If you look at the websites, a
lot of dominatrixes have wish lists up, stuff for these guys to buy them,
because the men like to do that. I mean, all the equipment I have was
given to me by different guys. And I have some very expensive things,
you know? They like to buy this stuff, they like for me to use it and take
care of it.

So nobody's coming over here to hurt me. Really. I had one stalker
once who was after me for years, but that was crazy. Nobody wants to
harm me. I have to go through a lot of crap to find the real people, so
many conversations that I have to have to get through to the real people.
Craigslist is a free-for-all. But if somebody calls you from something
like Eros Guide, you know that's probably a real one—they don't call
for no reason at all. Eros Guide is like the top, they have like the most
expensive escorts and dominatrixes in the country. Men who travel
around, businessmen that travel a lot can have a membership to Eros
and wherever they're going, they can book ahead of time and see who's
there. People still want to see somebody when they're traveling. That's
one of the best sites.

It's always been my dream to have my own dungeon. I did have
one for a while with my husband Michael. He advised me to become
a professional dominatrix, since I had all the equipment, costumes,
knowledge and the mind-set. He did, too. He and his friends fixed up the
house like a dungeon and my mother would serve my clients a cup of
coffee while they were waiting. Michael and I worked all the time, we
were very popular. We made plenty of money.

Makes the Ramones seem boring, doesn't it? So much more has

gone on in my life besides that. If I had stayed with Johnny, this never would've happened to me. I mean, I always thought about it but when I read *The Story of O*, all of a sudden a light went on in my head and it was like, now I know that there's nothing wrong with me and there are other people out there like me. Why I have these feelings. Why I like, and why I equate, violence with sex. A lot of people do.

I'll always want to have a dungeon. It's been a part of my life for so long. Everyone gets older but I don't think those tendencies ever go away. So what if my clients are older? They know me, and I have younger girls who want to be dommes, too.

I do not and never have hated men, nor was I molested or abused as a child. I naturally love the lifestyle, living and giving one's life for someone else. It's the ultimate—kind of like being a martyr or a saint. We are exorcists and keepers of others' demons. We are needed in this world.

# Notes

## 1975
"Performance Studios was on the second floor..." —Monte Melnick, email to emily xyz, 22 February 2005

## 1973–74–75
"Anya told me that Roxy..." —Eileen Polk, email to emily xyz, May 30, 2011

"The Village Plaza, 79 Washington Place..." —J. Anthony Lukas, "The Two Worlds of Linda Fitzpatrick"; *The New York Times*, October 16, 1967

1. "She wanted to go to California with the group and it just wasn't in the scheme of things with the managers. They weren't going to buy tickets for people's girlfriends. We'd just played ten shows at Max's, two a day, and I was very tired, stoned, been drinking all the time. I came home, it was very late and I went to sleep. I was lying face down and I heard something. She was standing on top of me holding a kitchen knife, so then I tried to stand up and take it away from her but she'd tied my ankles together. I tried to get the knife away from her and she cut my hand. Then I got mad so I thought whatever's going to happen, I have to get the knife away from her. I managed to wrestle it away but somehow in the process, I sliced my hand open and the bone was hanging out. The she, with no clothes, went out on the front fire escape [*of their apartment at First Avenue and 2nd St.*]. She was a great one for climbing out on the fire escape in the middle of winter with no clothes on [*although this particular incident took place in August*]. She had an outrageous body. This is the same girl who for kicks would take her clothes off and go out on the avenue and pretend she was hitchhiking, then watch the cars crash." —Arthur Kane, quoted in *The New York Dolls: Too Much Too Soon*, by Nina Antonia (1998: Omnibus Press), p. 90.

2. Built at the southeast corner of Fifth Avenue and Eighth Street in 1926 by developer Joseph G. Siegel, One Fifth Avenue was a type of building known as an "apartment hotel;" instead of conventional apartments or hotel rooms, it had two- and three-room suites, each with a "serving pantry" to which (originally) food was delivered by service elevator from a central restaurant on the ground floor. According to *The New York Times*, "the apartment hotel was a widespread fiction of the period; 'non-housekeeping' residential buildings could be built

taller and deeper than regular multiple dwellings because they were considered commercial buildings—[even though] tenants ... usually set up full kitchens in the serving pantries."  Christopher Gray, "Streetscapes: 1 Fifth Avenue: A Good Joke Not Well Retold," *The New York Times*, October 4, 1992.

3. Punk scenemaker Anya Phillips later managed No Wave band The Contortions and saxophonist James White, and was one of the founders of the influential Mudd Club.

"Anya was brilliant..." —Eileen Polk, email to emily xyz, May 30, 2011

4.  Anya Phillips can be seen wearing a similar shirt on the cover photo of Chris Stein's *Negative: Me, Blondie, and the Advent of Punk* (2014: Rizzoli)

"Malcolm was like..." —Peter Jordan, quoted in *The New York Dolls: Too Much Too Soon*, by Nina Antonia (1998: Omnibus Press), p. 162

"She took her name…" —Gyda Gash, email to Emily XYZ, August 29, 2012

5. "It was Anya Phillips who sold me my first G-string. I was sitting in a café and she came over and said, 'You should be a go-go girl. I make G-strings. I'll sell them to you.' I think she was interested in my being a go-go girl more as a source of revenue for her than anything else. But she said, 'Go to the Go-Go Agency.' So I did go, and a guy named Angel booked me around all five boroughs working the topless clubs. And I worked on 42nd Street for a time… in an extended run as Miss Monique. Look, it's a rather popular refrain these days, but I too am saddened by the loss of the seedy elements of New York. It's strange to take a cab down Disney-Second Street. I like to remember it as it was portrayed in films like Midnight Cowboy. But those days are gone. Manhattan's a different place now." —Monica Lynch, co-founder of Tommy Boy Records; interviewed 1999 by Steve LaFreniere for Index Magazine; indexmagazine.com

"It was a very free time…" —Gyda Gash, interview with emily xyz, September 13, 2006

6. *Do you remember when [Roxy and Johnny] started seeing each other?*
I do! I do, because it was just before I started seeing Cheetah [*Chrome*], and at that time it was kind of a free-for-all, like y'know, be with anybody you can. And she was with Johnny, screwing around with him, and it was like the informal, no-commitment relationship yet at that time. And she was also seeing Cheetah. She actually introduced me to the Dead Boys, brought me to my first Dead Boys show, and that's actually how I hooked up with Cheetah. I went with

her [to see] the Dead Boys, and I hooked up with Stiv [Bators] and she was with Cheetah, and then Cheetah saw me and we hooked up, and then she went back to Johnny—so after that we became couples. It's a little murky, but after that we were couples. Before that, it was kind of a free for all." —Gyda Gash, interview with emily xyz, September 13, 2006

7. Max's Kansas City, at 213 Park Avenue South in Manhattan, was owned and operated by Michael B. "Mickey" Ruskin from December 1965 until December 1974. The club was a legendary meeting-place for cultural figures including visual artists, musicians, politicians and actors. By the mid-70s, however, Ruskin—who allowed many of his regulars to run enormous tabs—could no longer sustain his operating expenses. He sold the business to Tommy Dean, who reopened it in late 1975, still as Max's Kansas City. This "second" Max's was one of the main performance venues for punk and new wave bands until it closed in 1981. Mickey Ruskin died May 16, 1983 of a cocaine overdose. The former Max's location, in a small building on Park Avenue South between 17th and 18th Streets, is now a restaurant, not (as is often published) a deli.

"Ashley's was a fancy..." —Eileen Polk, interview with emily xyz

"I found a 'Chicago' postcard..." —email from Eileen Polk, June 7, 2011

"I don't remember that Anya and Roxy..." —email from Eileen Polk, May 30, 2011

"By the time I met Roxy..." —email from Eileen Polk, May 30, 2011

"There were these two guys..." —Gyda Gash interview with emily xyz, September 13, 2006

## 1976
"Anya would always flirt..."—email from Eileen Polk, December 29, 2011

"Anya was hostile..." —email from Eileen Polk, May 30, 2011

"I remember the night they met at Max's..." —email from Eileen Polk, May 26, 2011

1. The Ramones played the Roundhouse in London on July 4, 1976, on a bill that included The Flamin' Groovies (first), Ramones (second), and Stranglers (third). The Ramones set list from that show:

1 - Loudmouth
2 - Beat On The Brat
3 - Blitzkrieg Bop
4 - I Remember You
5 - Now I Wanna Sniff Some Glue
6 - Glad To See You Go
7 - Gimme Gimme Shock Treatment
8 - 53rd & 3rd
9 - I Wanna Be Your Boyfriend
10 - Havana Affair
11 - Listen To My Heart
12 - California Sun
13 - Judy Is A Punk
14 - I Don't Wanna Walk Around With You
15 - Today Your Love Tomorrow The World

Their show at Dingwalls in London the following night was attended by members of the Sex Pistols, Clash and others, and probably followed much the same set list. Per  http://www.guitars101.com/forums/f90/ramones-1976-07-04-london-england-103422.html

"Roxy and I picked up Johnny..." —email from Eileen Polk, May 25, 2011

"I remember Johnny's ..."—Chris Frantz, drummer of Talking Heads, quoted in *Ramones: An American Band* by Jim Bessman, page 79

**"Roxy**, *that* chick..." —*New York Rocker* #4, Sept. 76; "Pressed Lips" by Janis Cafasso

"Roxy and I took the Long Island Railroad..." —email from Eileen Polk, June 7, 2011

"Outside CBGB..." —*New York Rocker #2,* March 1976, p. 16, Ramones essay by Stephen Anderson

2. The miniature black baseball bats were imprinted with the words "The Ramones - A Hit on Sire Records" (US) or "Ramones - Beat on the Brat" (UK). So far none of the UK version have surfaced, but the Ramones Museum in Berlin has one of the US bats on display. Per http://kauhajokinyt.fi/~jplaitio/gigs/CJGermanyMun3.html

Well, **Roxy** seems to have won her man... — *New York Rocker* vol. 1, No. 5, December 1976

3. "[Johnny Ramone's] estranged wife, Rosana Cummings, a hairdresser from Queens, recently won $75 a week alimony from Ramone, who has earned $6000 a week. She claimed in divorce papers that he made 'consistent and repeated demands [for her] to commit sexual acts with other men which caused [her] mental anguish, shame and humiliation.' " —*New York Post*, August 15, 1983. It should be noted that this was before no-fault divorce in New York State, where the only way to get a divorce was to allege something horrible about your spouse.

**Connie Ramone**'s legs... —*New York Rocker* vol. 1, No. 4, September 1976

"There are so many terrible stories..." —Ann Henderling, email to emily xyz, March 25, 2011. Ms. Henderling was a model and East Village resident in the 1980s.

"I heard Connie was from Fort Worth..." —email from Eileen Polk, June 7, 2011

"Connie definitely had a temper..." —Ann Henderling, email to emily xyz, March 28, 2011.

4. "As I remember the story, Connie came from Texas where she was married with [one child]. One day Connie couldn't take it anymore (I don't know why—too boring maybe). Anyway, she made dinner and left it in the oven, made some sort of arrangements for the baby, left a note for her husband who was not yet home from work, and she never went back. [She moved first to Los Angeles], I think this was probably in the mid- to late-[19]60s. [My friend who knew her] remembers Connie as very sweet in the 60s. I would not have called her 'sweet' by 1980.

"I never knew Connie in LA. I met [her] in [New York in] 1980. I was bored of LA, and Connie's best friend Pucci offered me a place to stay in Manhattan. [So] I left Malibu for New York and was living in a loft with Pucci and her boyfriend Melody Peach on East 9th St. and 2nd Avenue. One night I was alone (that hardly ever happened in this loft), doing my makeup in the bathroom, and the window went up, and there was Connie on the fire escape. She literally came in through the bathroom window—up the fire escape to our 5th floor loft. What's funny is that John Spacely (another NY character) [*and former boyfriend of Gyda Gash*] told me he met her the exact same way. She acted like this was totally normal. She said, 'HI! I'm Connie! Are you Annie? You're beautiful!!!'

"She said she wanted to borrow a belt from our friend Pucci. I was afraid to let her and afraid not to. She seemed tough and tall and urbane and about 1000 times cooler than I was, and she was a little scary. She was wearing really expensive fabulous boots, and when I admired them she told me she knew where I could get them wholesale for $300, but I'd have to let the salesman look up my skirt and I couldn't wear underwear. She thought this was a great deal.

"She took the belt because she had known Pucci longer than I had, and I was more scared of Connie than Pucci.

"[At that time s]he was in her 30s—Early 30s, cool and dangerous, reckless and exciting and rock and roll. She wore very intense makeup and had really pretty, thick, straight blonde hair. She told me she had no lines in her face and said it was because she never, ever, ever washed her face—she used only water. She put her face up next to mine and said "See, I look younger than you!!!" She didn't. She couldn't. I had just turned 20. She didn't look bad, but she didn't look 19." —Ann Henderling, email to emily xyz, March 25, 2011

"I didn't see Connie much..." —Eileen Polk, email to emily xyz, June 7, 2011

"Connie died of an overdose..." —email from Ann Henderling, March 25, 2011

"Then I was in Toronto..." —Dee Dee Ramone, *Lobotomy: Surviving the Ramones* (2000: DaCapo Press), pg. 192.

**Anya** (Ms Chow Mein)... —*New York Rocker,* vol. 1, no. 5, December 1976

"By early summer 1976..." —email from Eileen Polk, January 3, 2012

5. "Contortions Crack Up" by Tim Page, *New York Rocker*, vol. 1, no. 21, 1979 (no month / probably August), p. 12–13:

Pat Place: "Anya started pushing the band towards disco."

Jody Harris: "You know, I think she actually *hated* what we were doing. She wanted James to be a front man, and the band would stand behind him like disco cogs, doing nothing but playing parts. James White and the Blacks came out of this."

George Scott: "Anya had effectively separated herself and James from the rest of the band."

"The debut performance of James White and the Blacks, in February '79 at the Club 57, was but one of many memorable sets. ... I met Anya Phillips for the first time that same evening. [*he quotes from his own review of the show:*] 'After waiting thirty minutes in a freezing hallway for my reviewer's pass, I was finally ushered in by Ms. Phillips, who, as she stamped my hand, grabbed it with such ferocity that her half-inch painted nails drew blood...Any questions were met with total hostility."

George Scott: "She was such a terrible manager—and so cheap! She wouldn't give Pat Place $20 she owed her because she said Pat was onstage for less time than the rest of us!"

"Money was the cause of many of the musicians' problems with Anya Phillips. ... [T]he recording of the Contortions album was, by the ex-members' accounts, an intrapersonal disaster. ...

Don Christensen: "Sometimes we didn't even get paid. We did some live tracks for the soundtrack to Diego Cortez's *Grutzi Elvis*. Anya was given an advance by ZE Records. She took the check, smiled and said, 'I know who's *not* getting any of this.' And we didn't. She kept all the money. By this point, we felt like we were part of the Anya Phillips Show. We couldn't even talk to James anymore—Anya answered all the calls."

Jody Harris: "Finally, Anya got this guy to be her private secretary. We couldn't even talk to *Anya*. She'd just say, 'Oh, talk to my secretary!'" ...

Don Christensen: "ZE had wanted the whole band involved [in the recording of the Contortions' album], but Anya wouldn't hear of it. She called us shit, said we weren't needed. According to her, she had invented the Contortions' whole act... Anyway, Anya drew up a new contract where we were just considered 'session men,' and she and James were the band! So we broke up." ...

"Back in New York, rumors of the couple's growing preference for French heroin were running rampant. Chance seemed to be taking his emulation of the black jazz pioneers of the '50s to the limit, and some blamed Anya Phillips for pushing him to it."

*Sidebar interview with **James Chance**, p. 43, last question:*

**TP:** *Do you think your antagonism toward fans, the press, and the band members has damaged your career?*

JC: It's only helped my career! My career has been totally based on it. That's the basis of my success—anyone who thinks it's damaged my career is totally crazy! I mean, what career *was* there before I started antagonizing everyone?

**New York Rocker #22, September 1979:** Letter from Anya Phillips in Letters, p. 8: "It is apparent from the article that the reason for Mr. Page's poison pen goes back to a concert where he had not the professionalism to call prior to the show to be included on the press list, but chose instead to harass me, along with 600 others..." Tim Page replies: *I phoned Anya Phillips twice before the Club 57 show and was put off both times. Finally, I was told to show up at the door, which I did. ...*

**New York Rocker #24, November 1979:** Response from George Scott

(Contortions) to Anya Phillip's letter in #22, in Letters, p. 4 — "I was a
Contortion for over a year, and Anya contends that I only played eight gigs?
Sheesh!! ... Silly me—I'd believed that it was over a year of constant rehearsals,
gigs, auditions and practice that created a new sound and direction for rock and
roll. ... Anya's 'uncompromising behavior' split, shattered and destroyed an
uncompromising band."

"**Cheeter** and **Geeter** have jungle fever..."—New York Rocker vol. 1, no. 8,
July–August 1977, "Pressed Lips"

5. "At first I liked [Johnny] a lot, he was really fun, easy-going, yeeaah! He
became a pain in the ass later but he was much nicer [in the beginning], really
appreciative, really excited. He was more, like, square. He was in a relationship.
He was married! And he was cheating on her to see Roxy, which was a great
thrill for Roxy ... That really turned her on, the turn-on of being the Other
Woman. Anyway, he was really fun, and he loved us 'cause we were crazy
and acting out and he was very entertained, like, 'Oh, the clowns are going to
perform again!' That kind of a thing, but very nice and fun. And then he just,
it got more controlling as they became a couple."—Gyda Gash, interview with
emily xyz, 13 September 2006.

"Everyone has been commenting..." —*New York Rocker*, vol. 1, no. 5,
December 1976, "Pressed Lips"

6. Janis Cafasso wrote the "Pressed Lips" gossip column for *New York Rocker*,
and was the former girlfriend of New York Dolls/Heartbreakers guitarist Johnny
Thunders. Anna Sui is a well-known fashion designer. Abbijane Schifrin, also a
designer, died in New York on March 13, 2009, at age 50.

7. "Linda was a weird-looking little skank and she hung out with her fat friend
Anna Sui-pig, we called her—'SOOOEEEY-pig!' And those two would come
to CBGBs and they would have all kinds of frou-frouey outfits and, like, they
dressed *bad!* We were like, 'What the fuck?' Sui would pay, she had money, she
had a business. Walter Lure was living with her. He would take her money, buy
drugs, go shoot up at her house when she wasn't looking. Linda Danielle was
her sidekick. Those two. They were, like, people you wouldn't hang out with
and you were kind of like, *Eeew*."—Gyda Gash, interview with emily xyz

## 1977
**JOHNNY RAMONE** follows the yo-yo syndrome... and **DEE DEE
RAMONE**'s new year started off bleak... —both *New York Rocker*, vol. 1, no.

6, March 1977, "Pressed Lips" column

"[What] I remember about the stabbing…" email from Eileen Polk, May–June 2011

1. For Barbara Kane's account of the ass-stabbing incident, see her Epilogue to Arthur Kane's book, *I, Doll: Life and Death with The New York Dolls* (2009: Chicago Review Press), p. 210. She writes that the location was the "Washington Square Hotel," however, there was no Washington Square Hotel at that time. The Hotel Earle, located at 103 Waverly Place, was renovated and re-opened in 1986 as the Washington Square Hotel. The incident most likely took place at the Earle, where Dee Dee lived off and on, or possibly the Village Plaza, where Arthur had previously lived.

"Did any of you guys ever consider the military?" —*New York Rocker* #10, Nov–Dec 1977; p. 4-7. Ramones interview by Roy Trakin.

2. "I went to military school for two years" —Johnny Ramone, quoted in *Hey Ho Let's Go: The Story of the Ramones*, by Everett True (2002: Omnibus Press), footnote, p. 11.

3. "I didn't become bad until I got out of high school. Sniffing glue was probably the start of my downfall. My first drug experience was sniffing glue." —Johnny Ramone, interviewed by Timothy White; *Rolling Stone*, No. 284, February 8, 1979.

4. Arlene Kohn became the girlfriend of Mickey Leigh, brother of Joey Ramone, in 1976; they were married in 1982.

"I had my leather jacket since '67…" —Johnny Ramone, interviewed by Kim Cooper and Margaret Griffis for Scram #11, 2000 (month unknown); http://www.scrammagazine.com/tags/johnny-ramone

5. "More than two dozen record prices were set for movie posters for 'Casablanca', 'Citizen Kane', 'Frankenstein', 'Attack of the 50 Foot Woman' and other films in a public auction that included the movie poster collection of the late RAMONES guitarist Johnny Ramone. The $1 million auction was conducted Friday night, March 18, [2005], by Heritage Galleries of Dallas, Texas. ... Winning bidders paid a combined total of $1,047,267 for about 1,200 posters; about 150 of them from Ramone's personal collection,' said Grey Smith, Heritage's Director of movie poster auctions. ... '[Ramone's] superb collection contain[ed] some of the most sought-after titles in movie poster-

collecting, including 'Frankenstein' (1931), 'Bride of Frankenstein' (1935), 'Dracula' (1931), 'The Day the Earth Stood Still' (1951) and 'Forbidden Planet' (1956)," Smith added."— blabbermouth.net on roadrunnerrecords.com: http://legacy.roadrunnerrecords.com/blabbermouth.net/news. aspx?mode=Article&newsitemID=34516 ; and http://legacy.roadrunnerrecords. com/blabbermouth.net/news.aspx?mode=Article&newsitemID=29003


"[D]o you believe in jogging?" —*The Ramones: If All Men Were Brudders,* by Cynthia Rose; *Creem* Magazine, September 1983


6. [Johnny] despised all of Europe! Well, during my years with them anyhow. (laughs) He didn't like the food! When he was in England once he exploded at a sound check during a tour ... My partner, the late Linda Stein was with them then; I'd had to stay in New York. She called me just after this happened.

The Ramones were doing a sound check in some "shire" in England, and when you're touring the UK, you always got curry at sound check. Well, Johnny just wanted hamburgers, which is what he would get in America. By the way, the only places they ever played in America, before England, were New York, New Jersey and Boston, never more than 250 miles from New York. It was hard moving them out of home territory, nobody wanted them.

But in England, they were stars overnight! They were stars before they even got there. It was amazing. Still, like most bands you didn't get to choose the catering, you couldn't get lobster dinners, certainly not a hamburger during a sound check. This was before McDonalds, I don't think they knew what a hamburger was in Europe.

So Johnny yelled, "God Damn curry!!! Fucking curry!!! Why can't I get a hamburger!?!" As everybody knows, you didn't want to be around Johnny Ramone when he was angry. But Linda Stein said, "You know what, John? If you don't like it, then pick up your fucking guitar...get on a plane...and go FUCKING home!" ... Some spies of mine said it was the first time they ever saw Johnny Ramone with his tail between his legs...er, so to speak.

The punch line to this anecdote came many years later, when I was visiting Johnny and his wife Linda at their beautiful hillside house in some LA canyon. Johnny had been consulting the exterminator about dealing with 'mole holes' in the yard. They had just redesigned the kitchen, to Johnny's very specific specifications, and it was right out of Architectural Digest—[*laughs at the fact that badass Johnny Ramone had redesigned his kitchen*].

So I was there with Linda, and we were waiting to meet up with Rick Rubin and Eddie Vedder and John Frusciante for dinner, and Johnny says to me, "Hey Danny, there's this great Indian restaurant in Beverly Hills, really fantastic, we love it there, would you like to go?" Believe it!! The FUCKING-GOD-DAMN-CURRY Johnny Ramone opting to take everyone to vindaloo.

I loved John so much; he was one of the smartest people I ever knew, and one of the wisest as well. He drove a Cadillac, and he said that a kid came over to him in a parking lot and sort of snickered, "Hey, Johnny Ramone, a Cadillac isn't very punk, is it?" And Johnny answered, "Excuse me, I invented punk. If I drive a Cadillac, it's punk, OK?" —Danny Fields, Stay Thirsty website interview, part 2, August 2009 – http://www.staythirstymedia.com/200908-036/html/200908-danny-fields-pt2.html

"She loved it..." —Gyda Gash, interview with emily xyz

**Tommy:** Johnny didn't tell his parents... —*New York Rocker* #4, September 1976; p. 28, Interview with the Ramones by Lisa Persky, after their first trip to England (July 1976), with photos of the band in London by Danny Fields.

7. *New York Rocker* vol.1, no. 10, Nov–Dec. 1977, p. 4–7; Ramones interview by Roy Trakin, October 7, 1977, the day after they opened for Iggy Pop at the Palladium:

Are your parents proud of you?
**Johnny:** I don't know.
**Joey:** I let my mom come last night...
**Johnny:** My mother and father came for the first time last night.
First time?
**Johnny:** They couldn't hear, though, they said, "Isn't this bad for your hearing?" I called them up when I got home and they said: "My ears feel very funny. I can't hear anything."
**Joey:** My father once sat in front of John's amp.
Would you let your parents come to CBGB's?
**Joey:** Yeah, they've been there.
**Johnny:** Everyone else's have been to C.B.G.B.'s. I didn't want mine there cuz it's too...too...awful...very crowded there.
Do you feel inhibited when they're out there?
**Johnny:** N'yah, I don't think so...I forgot they were out there...I forgot everything that was going on last night.
Were you satisfied with last night's performance?
**Johnny:** Yeah.
What were some of the criticisms?
Bleeker Bob told me were weren't spread out enough...
**Dee Dee:** That's not what he told me...he thought we really filled the big stage quite well.
**Johnny:** No, but that's alright...I told him they only gave us one spotlight, so we hadda stand together.
I thought you looked real...vulnerable up there.
**Johnny:** It was a pressure situation...New York and all. ...

**Tommy:** Well, the situation is we weren't using our own stage, our own lights, our own PA…We were an opening act…it's a different situation when you're the top-billed act…

**Johnny:** The lighting man tells us the spots aren't working; the sound man tells us if you continue to play this loud you might as well bring your own PA to your next job, cuz you're not using this one.

"[Johnny's] parents wanted him…" —Tommy Ramone, quoted in *On The Road With The Ramones*, by Monte A. Melnick & Frank Meyer, p. 43

"My mom always treated me…" —Johnny Ramone, quoted in *On The Road With The Ramones*, by Monte A. Melnick & Frank Meyer, p. 41–43

"Johnny Ramone and I…" —Dee Dee Ramone, *Lobotomy: Surviving the Ramones* (with Veronica Kofman); (2000: Thunders Mouth Press), pgs. 73 & 47

"I wanted a guitar…" —Johnny Ramone, "Ramones: Cool by Proxy," by Craig Young, on http://www.earpollution.com/aug99/coolbyproxy/coolbyproxy.html

"We used to check out…" —Dee Dee Ramone, *Lobotomy: Surviving the Ramones*, p. 57

"I have never improved…" —Interview with Johnny Ramone by Joan Tarshis, *Guitar for the Practicing Musician,* November 1991; quoted in Jim Bessman, *Ramones: An American Band* (1993: St Martin's Press), p. 13

"Johnny…had a very low opinion…" Vera Ramone King, *Poisoned Heart: I Married Dee Dee Ramone* (2009: Phoenix Books), p. 50

**Johnny:** I was out of work… —Interview with the Ramones by Lisa Persky, *New York Rocker* vol. 1, no. 4, September 1976, p. 28

"How do you guys feel…" —*Trapped Backstage with the Ramones*, interview by emily xyz; *illiterature* (fanzine) no. 2, Herkimer NY, December 1977

"There was one incident…" —Vera Ramone King, *Poisoned Heart: I Married Dee Dee Ramone* (2009: Phoenix Books), p. 96

"Joey was a very lonely guy…" —Gyda Gash, interview with emily xyz, September 13, 2006

8. "Jeffrey Ross Hyman was born May 19, 1951, at Beth Israel Hospital in downtown Manhattan ... but the blessed day did not pass without extreme distress. The major encumbrance in my brother's life had actually formed before he'd ever taken his first breath. As nature would have it, a mass of what might have been another fetus that never developed had become attached to his spine. The medical term for the condition is 'sacrococygeal teratoma'; it describes a type of tumor with cells vastly different from the surrounding tissue. It occurs once every thirty-five to forty thousand births, with 75 percent affecting females. If the tumor is promptly removed, the prognosis is good. ... A few weeks later, when doctors deemed Jeff's tiny body strong enough to withstand the trauma of surgery, the procedure was successfully completed." —Mickey Leigh with Legs McNeil, *I Slept With Joey Ramone* (2009: New York, Touchstone/Simon & Schuster), p. 2.

"Johnny Ramone ... was the self-appointed..." —Vera Ramone King, *Poisoned Heart: I Married Dee Dee Ramone* (2009: Phoenix Books), p. 49–50

"Joey do you have any idea..." —*New York Rocker* #10, Nov–Dec 1977; Ramones interview

"[T]he Ramones used to torture Joey..." —Gyda Gash, interview with emily xyz, September 13, 2006

"Next night, at a folkie club in San Jose..." —*New York Rocker* vol. 1, no. 7, May–June 1977, "Pressed Lips"

"While **Little Linda** was snooping around..." —*New York Rocker* vol. 1, no. 8, July–August 77, "Pressed Lips"

"When **Phil Spector** saw **Dee Dee Ramone**..." —*New York Rocker* vol. 1, no. 8, July–August 77, "Pressed Lips"

"[T]here's this ancient story..." —Danny Fields, Stay Thirsty website interview, part 2

9. Linda Stein, wife of Seymour Stein, the president of Sire Records, co-managed the Ramones along with Danny Fields from 1975–1981. She later went on to become a successful "real estate agent to the stars" in New York City. She was murdered by her personal assistant on October 30, 2007.

## 1978

"Did Roxy ever talk about..." —Eileen Polk, email to emily xyz, May 27, 2011

"The mystery of Roxy's murder..." —*New York Rocker* vol. 1, no. 11, February–March 1978 [issue says 1977 – typo], "Pressed Lips"


## 1979

"Baby I Love You' is a black mark..." —Johnny Ramone, *Scram* issue #11, 2000 (no month), by Margaret Griffis and Kim Cooper

"Monte came to meet me..." —Johnny Ramone, quoted in *On The Road With The Ramones*, by Monte A. Melnick & Frank Meyer, p. 176

"The Rattlers were playing..." —Mickey Leigh, *I Slept with Joey Ramone* (Touchstone: 2009), pg. 202

"We played with the Ramones..." —Nikki Corvette, quoted in *Detroit Rock City: The Uncensored History of Rock'n'Roll in America's Loudest City*, by Steve Miller (Da Capo: 2013), p. 193


## 1980

"Each day of our European..." —Vera Ramone King, *Poisoned Heart,* p. 54

"In the beginning, it was all about..." —Gyda Gash, interview with emily xyz. September 13, 2006

"The first time we kissed..." —Johnny Ramone, quoted in *I Slept with Joey Ramone*, p. 208

"I got this card..." —Johnny Ramone, *The Ramones: If All Men Were Brudders,* by Cynthia Rose; *Creem* Magazine, September 1983

"John was always..." —Dee Dee Ramone, *Lobotomy: Surviving the Ramones*, p. 56

"I was a fan like everybody...." —Johnny Ramone, quoted in "Johnny Ramone on the Vagrants – An Interview by Mike Stax," on http://www.rockforever.com/singers/west/vagrants.html


## 1981

1. Simon Reynolds, *Rip It Up and Start Again: Post-Punk 1978–1984* (Penguin: 2006), p. 21-22

2. "There's A Riot Goin' On: The Infamous Public Image Ltd. Riot Show at the Ritz, 1981"—Interview with Ed Caraballo (video/lighting designer), July 1997; on Perfect Sound Forever, http://www.furious.com/perfect/pil.html. The drummer for this notorious gig, Sam Ulano, is a well-known New York session regular and drum instructor. Jeannette Lee was a longtime Lydon associate who went on to manage Rough Trade Records.

3. "[W]hen I moved into Needles Jones' loft [at 317] Bowery in 1983, I discovered several boxes of [Anya's] clothing and accessories tucked in a corner. ... The loft had previously been the residence of a great many rock legends including Tuxedo Moon and contained many similar forgotten or 'stored' items. And since neither Needles nor I felt it was a priority to pay the tiny rent on the space, all of those historic items were left behind upon eviction." —Hattie Hathaway; "At some point all her stuff ended up at my loft ... James came by to get some of the things." —Needles Jones; "Chris Stein has Anya's ashes under his bed. At least that's what he told me." —Johnny Dynell; all from motherboards.com.

"He would go on these walks..." —Gyda Gash, interview with emily xyz, September 13, 2006

"I knew from the get-go!..." —Gyda Gash, interview with emily xyz, September 13, 2006

4. *[H]e was also attracted to Linda, though, don't you think?*
She was not that attractive! No, as I said, I think it was a combination of Linda's persistence and the fact that he was taking something away from Joey, and it would torture Joey. Whether this is conscious or not, [I don't know]. You never know what attracts you to somebody. I mean, she was a mousey, annoying, loud voice—not the type of person that you'd think he would be attracted to! If anything, you would think if he's gonna dump her, dump her for somebody grand! He could have *gotten* somebody grand! Why is he choosing *this?* —Gyda Gash, interview with emily xyz, September 13, 2006

"She did it out of respect for their relationship..." —Gyda Gash, interview with emily xyz, September 13, 2006

## 1982

"If there was a big party..." —Gyda Gash, interview with emily xyz, September 13, 2006

"I dunno if we had fun together..." —Johnny Ramone, quoted in "Johnny Ramone Looks Back At The Ramones" by Jenny Tatone; neumu.net, February 6, 2003

## 1983
"Some people were a bit concerned..." —Eileen Polk, email to emily xyz  May 30, 2011

"I had seen her many times with JR..." —Johnny Angel, email to emily xyz, January 11, 2006

1. "[P]sycho-phant, is that the word? ... Sicko-phant. Yeah. ... She might have had an affair with him back in the day, and [he was] obsessed with her and he would send me these e-mails. He's married, he's got two kids now, and he goes on the internet and keeps track of her prison record, keeps track of everything—it's creepy. And he's creepy." —Gyda Gash, interview with emily xyz, September 13, 2006

"Jealous Rage..." —Associated Press (wire), August 16, 1983

"I got the call the next day..." —Gyda Gash, interview with emily xyz, September 13, 2006

3. *What can you tell me about the incident w/ Seth Macklin?*
She met him (Seth) in a bar, JR came back to 85 E10, saw them on the street talking, yelled at her, hit Macklin with his gear bag, Macklin "curb jobbed" him. I was blamed for this by some, until I pointed out I was 215 miles away at the time. —Johnny Angel, email to emily xyz, January 11, 2006

## 1984–89
1. X-Man, posted 4-30-2006: "What ever became of Cindy Whitney, aka Roxie Ramone? She had bleached blonde hair, drank a lot, and lived with Johnny Ramone in New York, from the mid-70s to the mid-80s. After she came back to Chicago, she hung out at Dreamerz and Exit with Tomahawk, James Mean, red-haired Scotty (R.I.P), Cara, and "sick" Bill Edmondson. She drove a pink 50s Cadillac, and was a total wing nut! Very intense, and hot!"
Tomahawk, posted 6-27-2006: "It was a red 1972 eldorado with a white convertible. Yeah it was a cool car."
Tomahawk, posted 7-2-2006: "After she left Johnny he would buy her condos or pay for her rent wherever she would go next."
X-Man, posted 7-11-2006: "She and Bill were old high school buddies, if I remember right. She also used to tell us all these bizarre stories about this apartment she and Bill had in Hollywood when they both got out of high school in the early 70s, where they hung out with the Dolls and the G.T.O.s."
neo2000, posted 7-12-2006: "I never knew this girl, either, but she sounds great! If she was ever involved with James or Edmondson, she must be a real piece of work! ... fuck 'End Of The Century,' let's do a movie about her!" — www.windycitypunk.com, MIAs/RIP bulletin board

2. "I remember Gail's death vividly. She had come up to Boston to see [my band] the Blackjacks play a show at the Rat [*Boston's foremost punk venue, in Kenmore Square*] with Chris Spedding. She arrived on a Thursday. Thursday night, she spent with Rafe [*Raphael Mabry, rhythm guitarist*] and they did heroin together, she wasn't used to the strength of the dosage and died in his bathroom. He called me that Friday, destroyed. My roommate Julie and I babysat him and I told him that if he couldn't play, no problem (we'd been a trio before he had joined). However, I told him, no outbursts, just do it and we got on with it. There was a ballad in the middle of the set called "My Soul Flame" (inspired, naturally, by Cynthia). He broke down and sobbed at the beginning of it—it was heavy. That was spring 1984." —Johnny Angel, email to emily xyz, 31 August 2012

3. "[M]y encounters with [Johnny Ramone] in person had been strained and ugly since Cynthia had revealed to him (maybe in '84?) that we'd had a thing ... [T]he Blackjacks had seen firsthand how bad this rift was when we did a show in Hampton Beach [*New Hampshire*] with the Ramones in 1986 [*June 22*]— when JR had found out whom the opener was, he'd had Monte and their crew move their stuff FORWARD so we'd have nowhere to stand onstage. Thing is, the owner of the joint and my manager had been friends forever and the owner told them to move their stuff back or go home to New York. So, he was even angrier than he would have been under ordinary circumstances (ironically, once it became apparent that my presence was making him crazy, Joey and DeeDee became umpteen times friendlier!). Also, he and I were calling Cynthia back in Chicago one after the other, him telling her, "His band sucks, they're Spinal Tap," me telling her, "What the fuck is that douchebag's problem?" while we were within 50 feet of each other."—Johnny Angel, email to emily xyz, 30 August 2012

## 1990–98

1. Roxy might have gone back to Chicago, but she [would] still come to New York, she was very good friends with my friend Chris Skleros. I remember one time meeting her there at his apartment and, phone call—it's Johnny. I'm like: "It's *Johnny?* You guys are broken up for like 4 years, what the fuck is he calling—" Oh no: he still calls; pays the rent; still wants to know what is she doing, who's she talking to, what'd she do ... And it went on and on and on, phone calls 1-2-3-4-5 times a day. So while he was with Linda, he was doing the same thing that he was doing with Roxy, doing the other-woman thing he did with Linda, with *her*.

***Do you think that Linda ever knew that?***
If she didn't know that, she's a fucking moron. She must have known, but she probably—you know, she had the paper and God knows what, so she probably was satisfied, or who—I don't want to read that person's mind.

But this thing that they had in a perverse way was more satisfying, because she was the Other Woman. The one who got the attention, the secret. And that is almost more precious than the stable relationship—the relationship you're out with. The one you're secretly seeing, your secret desire, your secret passion, seemed to turn her on more. —Gyda Gash, interview with emily xyz, September 13, 2006

"Johnny knew for a long time…" —*The Ramones*, by Rick Johnson, on http://www.penduluminc.com/MM/articles/ramones.html

"I wanted to find a place…"—Johnny Ramone, interviewed by Kim Cooper and Margaret Griffis for Scram #11, 2000 (month unknown); http://www.scrammagazine.com/tags/johnny-ramone

## 2003–04

"Once every few weeks…" —Johnny Ramone, quoted in "Rock n Roll Loses Its Toughest Soldier," by Frank Meyer, *LA City Beat* #68

1. "I got there about five, six days before [Johnny] died. Maybe a week before, he's very ill by then. And I was talking on the phone with him all the time. Basically pleading to see him, and for whatever reasons he didn't want to see me. With him I guess it was a combination of many things, but one of them possibly being, again, since I never saw him very ill, maybe he didn't want me to see him in that condition. I think, because he could have passed away at any time at that point, because that's the stage his illness was at, he seemed to want to be surrounded by his new friends, who were all celebrities.

"And this for some reason was very important to him. I think he considered it a sign of achievement or of winning the prize of being successful by having celebrity friends, I guess. This is very important to him. Winning and achievement were everything to him. Everything was a game to him and he had to win it all. If you noticed the press release of his death, it says he was surrounded by…you know the names, big names. … [I]t was important to him, for whatever reason. …

"[E]ven at the Rock'n'Roll Hall of Fame, Johnny had his own table, with his celebrities. … He didn't have any Ramones at his table. … I think he wanted to separate himself, put himself in another league or something. … [Before he died] I was in Los Angeles, just a couple of miles away from where he lives… we had closure over the phone. And I said, 'C'mon I wanna go see you.' He said, 'Nah, nah.' We knew we were close, you know, we bonded over the phone. But it was strange, really strange. He had to play his game all the way to the end. He had to win, whatever that means. I don't know, I mean, I certainly didn't think he won anything, but in a way that made me feel good. That he left thinking that he won, which was very important to him. That made me feel great because what he had to go through was unbelievable. I felt so bad for him. I mean it was just so awful what happened to him. So I felt good about that, that he felt like he left a winner." —Tommy Ramone, "All The Angles Are True," interview by John Piccarella, January 23, 1005; on Perfect Sound Forever, www. perfectsoundforever.com/v/2005014/features/116

"You live in New York..." —Linda Ramone, interviewed on Fox News *Red Eye*, January 2005

2. "A bitter battle over Johnny Ramone's estate has pit Stella Cummings, the 79-year-old mother of the legendary guitarist, against his wife, Linda Cummings.

"Stella Cummings claims that Johnny, who died in September of prostate cancer, had promised her $2,500 a month, but she suspects Linda somehow convinced the punk rock pioneer to leave her out of his will.

"'I think she got him to change the will when he was sick, but I don't have any proof,' Stella tearfully told Page Six. 'It's been one big nightmare for me. Two weeks before my son passed away, he said, "Linda will send you a check every week." I haven't received a penny from her. And she's used foul language to me. It's disgusting. She said, "You'll never get a penny of this money." It's not her money, it's my son's money. She can't give me something to survive on?'

"Stella, who works as a cashier at a supermarket in Florida, is especially upset because Linda did not invite her to Johnny's cremation service.

"'That's my son!' Stella wailed. 'And I was close to my son. I was never told about it...Johnny was stupid to trust her to do what's right. She's like a vulture.'

"But when we reached Linda at her Los Angeles home, she offered no apologies. 'Everyone always leaves everything to their wife,' Linda said. 'Her son made every decision, and everyone who knew Johnny Ramone knows that. No one ever told him anything. She wasn't left anything in the will. That was her son's choice, not mine.

"'She has every bit of information from my estate lawyer to her estate lawyer,' Linda continued. 'If she can't accept his decision, that's her problem. It's very sad that she called a newspaper about this. Johnny was such a private person and I know he's looking down at her and saying, "This is disgraceful."

"'It is really despicable and disgusting to do this to him. It's my money and Johnny's money. Johnny Ramone would be livid if he knew his mother was doing this. We are private people. She should get on with her own life and stop being a RAMONES groupie.'

"This isn't the first time that Linda has been a source of contention between Johnny and someone close to him. Johnny became irrevocably estranged from fellow band member Joey Ramone when Linda, who was then Joey's girlfriend, left him for Johnny, whom she married in 1994.

"Johnny and Joey went on playing together for years, but still weren't speaking to each other when Joey died of cancer in 2001." —*The New York Post*, Page Six, December 23, 2004

244

Notes

"GALLO BACKS RAMONE WIDOW

"AFTER reading our story yesterday about the battle between the late Johnny Ramone's 79-year-old mother, Stella Cummings, and his widow, Linda Cummings, over the legendary guitarist's estate, filmmaker Vincent Gallo sprang to Linda's defense. Gallo, who described Johnny as 'the closest friend I've ever had in my life,' said his cancer-stricken pal never intended to leave Stella any money, and shot down her claims that Linda influenced Johnny's decision. 'First of all, he knew he was ill for seven years,' Gallo said. 'He'd been talking about and plotting his will for a long time. His logic was that his mother had a quarter-million in the bank, she's 79 years old, and giving her any more money would only be given to the government when she passed away.'

"Gallo added that Johnny and his mother weren't on the best of terms: 'It was Johnny Ramone who in a very clear state of mind said he didn't want his mother visiting him and he didn't want her at his bedside. I think it's outrageous that his mother is now making claims that Linda mistreated her.'" —*The New York Post*, Page Six, December 24, 2004


"Pete Yorn, John Frusciante and Eddie Vedder..." —"Rock & Roll Cemetery," by Dan Kapelovitz; *LA Weekly*, January 21–27, 2005


3. Tommy Ramone also died at the relatively young age of 65 in 2014, of cancer.


**2010**
"Rob Zombie explained..." —"Rock & Roll Cemetery," by Dan Kapelovitz; *LA Weekly*, January 21–27, 2005


1. "The making of friends, who are real friends, is the best token we have of a man's success in life." —Edward Everett Hale


**EPILOGUE: DOMINATRIX**
1. Possibly refers to the death of Michael Lord, 53, who died in July 2000 in a New Hampshire dungeon. The dominatrix, Barbara Asher, was acquitted in 2009.

# About the Authors

**Cynthia "Roxy" Whitney** was at the center of the downtown rock scene in New York from the time she arrived in 1974 at age 17. Along with her friend Anya Phillips, she helped create the bondage-inspired, extreme style that became famous as the "punk" look. Her social circle included, and brought together, many underground musicians and artists of mid-70s New York. She was also Johnny Ramone's girlfriend during the first and most influential phase of the band's career. She lives in Los Angeles.

**Emily XYZ** is a writer, spoken-word performer, and Ramones fan. She is the author of *The Emily XYZ Songbook: Poems for 2 Voices*. Her work appears in numerous anthologies, including *Aloud: Voices from the Nuyorican Poets Cafe*, and *Up is Up but So is Down: New York's Downtown Literary Scene, 1974–1992*. She lives in Saratoga Springs, New York.

Printed in November 2021
by Rotomail Italia S.p.A., Vignate (MI) - Italy